Superheroes:
An Analysis of Popular Culture's
Modern Myths

D1485235

By
David Reynolds

Superheroes: An Analysis of Popular Culture's Modern Myths
by David Reynolds ©2008, 2011, 2013

A thesis submitted to the School of Graduate Studies in partial fulfillment of the requirements for the degree of Master of Philosophy in Humanities, Memorial University of Newfoundland

December 2008

St. John's, Newfoundland

ISBN-13: 978-1477422076

ABSTRACT

A semiotic and cultural anthropological interrogation of popular North American superhero narratives, such as those of Superman, Spider-Man, and Batman, provides insight into how media's messages influence the culture's ethical values. Since emerging in the late 1930s, the superhero has become a pervasive figure in North American popular culture. As an extension of ideas presented by Friedrich Nietzsche, Joseph Campbell, and Umberto Eco, this dissertation argues that superhero tales must be regarded as modern mythology. It follows that people observe and learn social norms of justice from such narratives, since these ideals are intrinsic to the tales. In investigating the superhero's role as a contemporary figure of myth, this project focuses primarily on three areas: an account of the history of the superhero from 1938 to present; an examination of the cultural functions of contemporary superhero narratives; and, an interrogation of vigilantism, responsibility, and justice in these narratives and how those concerns further relate to ideologies and practices in North American culture.

3

ACKNOWLEDGMENTS

While this dissertation is a product of my own research over the past two years, it would not have been completed without the guidance and support of people very close to me. First, I would like to thank Dr. Chris Lockett, my supervisor, for being there to listen to my ideas and for encouraging me to always dig deeper. Without his guidance, this project would not have the breadth and fullness that it strives to achieve. Second, I need to express my gratitude to Dr. Jennifer Dyer, the Humanities Program's lecturers, and my fellow Humanities students. My experiences, both in class and out, have been exciting, intriguing, and thoroughly educational. Third, I am grateful to the School of Graduate Studies, the Graduate Students' Union, the Humanities Program, Dr. Brad Levett, and Dr. Arthur Sullivan for the financial support throughout my graduate studies. Without your aid, I would not be pursuing this Master's degree. Finally, I must thank my family, friends, and loved ones. My parents, Clyde and Bernice, have given me more support and faith than I can express with words. I can only say thank you, and hope to make you proud. My sisters, Paula and Denise, have always encouraged and inspired me. One day, I hope to return the favour. Thank you. My friends, in particular, Lee, Amanda, Nick, and Jessica, helped me blend my research with my leisure, making my research a joy. And, my girlfriend, Stephanie… thank you for your questions, your patience, your humour, your insight, your company, your shoulder, and your love. Thank you. Thank you all for your enthusiasm, encouragement, and support throughout my graduate studies. I cannot thank you enough.

CONTENTS

LIST OF ILLUSTRATIONS

INTRODCUTION

The Superhero as Modern Myth

The Superhero as Modern Myth

Interrogating how the superhero tale functions as a modern form of myth provides insight into both the ethical values of North American culture and the cultural influence of media's messages. The cultural function of mythic heroes such as those from Greek, Roman, and Norse cultures has attracted significant scholarly attention. Yet, what is the relevance of those ancient heroes today, and what are we to make of their hitherto academically neglected modern equivalents, popular superhero figures, such as Superman, Spider-Man, and Batman? A culture's prominent narratives become that culture's myths, reinforcing cultural values and disseminating norms of social behaviour. Joseph Campbell asserts that myths in modernity are not carriers of religious content, but of political and economic organization (Campbell 387). That is, modern myths need not be founded upon religious ideologies; rather, such myths develop from ethical perspectives as they relate to a political and economic world. In North America, superhero tales have become a significant part of the culture's myths, providing potent messages of right and justice. A semiotic and cultural anthropological interrogation of popular North American superhero narratives, such as those of Superman, Spider-Man, and Batman, offers insight into how media's messages influence the culture's ethical values.

Since emerging in the 1930s, tales of superheroes have transcended comics, branching out into radio, television, film, and music (Morris ix). They are now a pervasive aspect of North American popular culture. Friedrich Nietzsche asserts that a culture has no more powerful unwritten laws than those presented in its myths (Nietzsche 110). If the superhero tales of the twentieth century are understood as myths, then it follows from Nietzsche's assertion that people observe and learn social norms of justice from iconic superhero characters such as Superman, Spider-Man, and Batman, because these ideals are intrinsic to the tales. Roland Barthes further holds that myth gives a natural justification to a historical intention (Barthes 155). Accordingly, the superhero tale's social function is to validate certain ideals of justice in a historical and social context, naturalizing conventional values in a society. During the 1940s and 50s, Frederic Wertham, a child psychiatrist specializing in juvenile delinquency, spearheaded the crusade against comics, increasing public awareness of the influence of media's messages on people. Despite Wertham's "sensationalized portrait of the worst that comic books had to offer" (Beaty 93), media's effect on a culture's perspectives and the individual's outlook ought to remain a primary concern in cultures constantly bombarded by messages. In investigating the superhero's role as a modern mythical figure, my project focuses primarily on three areas: a synopsis of the history of the superhero tale from 1938 to the present; an examination of the cultural functions of contemporary superhero tales; and, an interrogation of the superhero's persistent issues and concerns, including not only vigilantism, responsibility, and justice, but also how those issues further relate to ideologies and practices in North American history.

In a close critical analysis of the myth structures of superhero tales, it is necessary to closely analyze the theories of myth found in texts such as Barthes' *Mythologies*, Nietzsche's *The Birth of Tragedy*, Umberto Eco's *A Theory of Semiotics*, and Joseph Campbell's *The Hero with a Thousand Faces*. I apply these theories to a critical reading of selected superhero tales presented in comics, television, and film, taking into account the difference of each medium on the myth's function. I further apply these analyses to the cultural conventions represented and how they are naturalized through the telling of superhero tales.

Here, I wish to establish briefly how contemporary iconic superheroes can be understood to reflect the moral conventions of North American popular culture, such as common beliefs about duty and justice. Externalist theories of mythology regard myth as providing a justification for social customs. This leads to the functionalist approach that I take, which follows from both Plato's and Malinowski's perspectives on myth. Their perspectives are externalist in the sense that they engage myth as "essentially interpretations of the external world," as opposed to internalist interpretations which take myth as "spontaneous expressions of the human mind" (Harris 43). Superheroes like Superman and Batman fulfill a strikingly similar social function to that of mythical heroes, such as Heracles and Odysseus. The similar externalist views of Plato and Malinowski apply to the mythic heroes as well as to superheroes and to the function of these narratives in culture. Through the functionalist perspective of myth, I argue that the superhero narratives of Superman and Batman function as moral charters.

In order to appreciate the significance of ancient myth, we ought to consider how ancient scholars would interpret them. As such, in order to better represent the perspectives of Ancient Greece, I engage Plato's treatment of myth in the *Republic*. The *Republic* is an attempt to define justice through the hypothetical construction of an ideal state though dialectic. In constructing the ideal state, Socrates and his interlocutors discuss the role that myth will have in the education of children. Here, it is unmistakable that Plato recognizes myth's function as an educational tool in society. In the *Republic*, Socrates says to the others that "we begin by telling children [myths], and the [myth] is,

10

taken as a whole, false, but there is truth in it also" (Plato 377a). Plato also emphasizes

that, in youth especially, mythic tales make an impression on a person's character (Plato

377b), making it clear that Plato holds that myths influence moral character. This is

further evident in the effort Socrates and his companions spend in encouraging rigorous

censorship of mythic tales of gods and heroes. Socrates claims that, in education, "we

must begin… by a censorship over our story-makers, and what they do well we must pass

and what not, reject" (Plato 377c). He also suggests that mothers and nurses will be

induced to tell these acceptable tales to their children "and so shape their souls by these

stories" (Plato 377c).

Janet E. Smith's article, "Plato's Use of Myth in the Education of Philosophic

Man," also emphasizes that Plato held mythic tales to be significant tools in teaching

morality. According to Smith, mythic tales constitute nearly the entirety of the

"intellectual" education of ordinary people (Smith 22). Thus, Socrates endeavours to

ensure that the content of myth is in accordance with the truth (Smith 22). She also goes

so far as to claim that the *Republic* "in every way gives the impression that there is much

to learn from the myths – and that those who do philosophy should not discount them"

(Smith 23). According to the presentation of myth in Plato's *Republic*, it appears that

ancient philosophers were not blind to myth's influence on the moral education of the

populace. Rather, Plato recognizes that mythic tales should be moulded to the purpose of

fostering virtuous character.

However, since Plato does not reflect exclusively upon myth's function in society,

we should also consider a more contemporary approach to interpreting mythic tales.

Malinowski, an influential figure in early 20th century anthropology, provides contemporary insight into Plato's theory in his charter theory of myth. A concise account

of Malinowski's charter theory of myth comes from his 1926 article, "Myth in Primitive

Psychology." There, Malinowski claims that "myth fulfills in primitive culture an

indispensable function: it expresses, enhances, and codifies belief; it safeguards and

enforces morality; it vouches for the efficiency of ritual and contains practical rules for

the guidance of man" ("Myth in Primitive Psychology" 82). For Malinowski, myth is

essentially a charter of belief, ritual, and ethics ("The Foundations of Faith and Morals"

139), and "the function of myth… is to strengthen tradition and endow it with a greater

value" ("Myth" 114).

Ivan Strenski, in his Introduction to *Malinowski and the Work of Myth*, provides a

straight forward application of the charter theory of myth in the Christian myth of Adam

and Eve. He claims that "the story has functioned in the past, among other things, to

charter the institutions of wearing clothes, bearing children in pain, or working by the

'sweat of our brows'" (Strenski xvii). Now, the myths functioning within a culture need

not all originate from religious thought. Instead, as Strenski acknowledges, Malinowski

asserted that "myth functions unconsciously as far as the actors in question are

concerned" (Strenski xvii). Accordingly, people do not necessarily consciously reflect

upon the lessons of myth; rather, the lessons of the tales become second nature and

people unwittingly comply with them. Strenski also draws attention to the fact that "early

in his career, Malinowski argued that only so-called 'primitive' culture" was susceptible

to his charter theory of myth; however, in his later career, he applied his theories to more

modern cultures' myths as well (Strenski xviii). Malinowski's charter theory of myth

expands upon Plato's perspective on myth. Whereas Plato recognizes the influence of

12

myth as an educational tool, Malinowski further acknowledges that myth functions not only as a moral instructor, but in justifying specific institutions, as well.

It appears as if Plato and Malinowski share very similar accounts of myth. Both hold that mythic tales teach moral lessons to the people of a culture. Now, let us consider how this perspective on myth illuminates the mythic heroes, Heracles and Odysseus. First, let me introduce our mythic heroes. Heracles is a hero of Ancient Greece. He is the son of the god Zeus and the mortal Alcmene. Furthermore, Heracles is generally known as one of the strongest of all Greek heroes, and he is best known for the Twelve Labours imposed on him by King Eurystheus. Eventually, Heracles was rewarded with immortality on Olympus (Harris 1056). Odysseus, on the other hand, is the son of Laertes and Anticleia, husband of Penelope, father of Telemachus, King of Ithaca, and favourite of Athene. He was celebrated for his prudence, ingenuity, and resourcefulness. Odysseus engineered the fall of Troy and, as the hero of Homer's *Odyssey*, he demonstrated endurance and adaptability that determined his successful return to Ithaca.

How are we to understand the possible functions of these ancient mythic heroes? In general, Heracles can be interpreted as endorsing strength and bravery. In particular, perhaps the most important function of Heracles' mythic tales is the underlying message of the Twelve Labours. Heracles is sent upon the Twelve Labours as a means of repentance for sinning against his family. The family was central in the foundation of government in Ancient Greece. Thus, the family, or *oikos*, was a valuable institution that helped maintain the status quo of the state in Ancient Greece. The Twelve Labours of Heracles function as a charter encouraging respect for maintaining the family for the good of the state because the tale acts as a warning for others. Odysseus, on the other

13

hand, is not a model of strength like Heracles; instead he represents intelligence and cunning. In his journey in the *Odyssey*, the tale appears to function as a charter of the Greek customs of *xenia*, or guest hospitality. There are numerous occasions in the *Odyssey* where those who abuse hospitality customs later suffer greatly, such as the Cyclops, Polyphemus, or Penelope's suitors upon Odysseus' return to Ithaca. The customs of guest hospitality were sanctioned by Zeus himself, and they were an important convention of life in Ancient Greece. The *Odyssey* can be seen to function as a charter for *xenia* in Ancient Greece. In both of these cases, the myths function to support significant aspects of Ancient Greek culture. While these tales reinforce the *oikos* and *xenia*, they also operate on the level of duty and justice. These tales emphasize that people have a duty to maintain the *oikos* and *xenia*, and if they cannot uphold their duties, then justice will be dealt upon them.

I argue that the tales and adventures of Superman and Batman, function as chartering certain elements of North American culture just like the ancient hero myths. In order to explain this, I should briefly introduce our superheroes. Superman is the last survivor of the planet Krypton, sent to earth as an infant. As a Kryptonian on Earth, Superman is gifted with an array of superpowers ranging from superstrength to x-ray vision. Raised by the "everyman" Kent family on a farm in Smallville, Superman was raised to embody the ideal American norms of honesty and justice. As a superhero, Superman is dedicated to "truth, justice, and the American way." Batman, on the other hand, witnessed the murder of his millionaire parents as a young child, and swore an oath dedicating his life to fight crime. He is at the peak of human physical and intellectual performance. While fighting crime, Batman utilizes a vast array of gadgetry, such as his batbelt, batarangs, and the batmobile. He represents the epitome of human physical fitness and intellectual conditioning and, by extension, he symbolizes how people may unlock their true potential through will and determination. Already, Batman and Superman begin to appear similar to their ancient predecessors insofar as that they act as examples or role models.

Both of these comic book characters come into being in the late 1930s, and, during World War II, their tales exhibit an obvious function in Malinowski's sense. During the war, both Superman and Batman stories were used to encourage support for the war effort.[1] Ian Gordon claims in his article, "Comic Books During World War II: Defending the American Way of Life," that Superman and Batman were basically "salesmen for the war effort" (Gordon 74). He also explains that "although the comic books encouraged the purchase of war bonds and supported paper, rubber, and metal salvage drives, writers and artists continued to present the United States as a consumer society with a bright future" (Gordon 77). Additionally, he writes that most Batman stories of the time upheld the honest acquisition of commodities, while denouncing criminal consumer desire (Gordon 78), and Superman tales were linking patriotism to legitimate business, while Superman thwarts illicit business (Gordon 79). During WW II, Superman and Batman functioned as a charter for supporting the war effort and for upholding the "American way" of consumerism.

However, the current function of Superman and Batman tales is not so blatant. In his book, *Superman on the Couch*, Danny Fingeroth explains that:

> Superheroes generally agree that the laws of the land need to be upheld. They believe that democracy is the best form of government. They believe in racial, religious, and gender parity; judge each individual on his or her own merits. In other words, without

---

[1] This matter is examined in more detail later in Chapter 2, "Superheroes and the World War II Propaganda Monologue."

being overtly ideological, superheroes champion the consensus views of most residents of Western democracies. (Fingeroth 160)

We can also observe from Superman and Batman tales that they strongly encourage reforming criminals (consider how Batman consistently leaves repeat offenders in the hands of the law, where they then end up in Arkham Asylum). In their earlier stories, Superman and Batman tales functioned as charters for patriotic duty and capitalist ideals. Today, they also charter broader, democratic ideals such as equality and criminal reform. Their stories both foster a sense of duty to uphold these institutions and relate moral guidance through the character's sense of justice. Notice that, both during World War II and today, the tales of superheroes like Superman and Batman act as legitimizing forces for the underlying foundations of society. Superhero tales help to reinforce these cultural institutions in the collective unconscious.

Superhero tales function as tools for moral education in the same manner as Plato and Malinowski interpreted myth. Just as the mythic tales of Heracles and Odysseus reinforce Ancient Greek institutions, so do our superhero tales reinforce North American democratic ideals. While the institutions reinforced by these tales differ from one era and culture to another, they nonetheless function to unconsciously support the institutions of a culture. It appears that both Plato and Malinowski would interpret these iconic superhero narratives in the same way they regarded myth. Thus, since they both serve the same function, superhero tales function as modern myths within North American culture and must be studied as such.

However, myths are much more complex than simple charters for cultural institutions. That myths might serve as a popular means of supporting cultural values is just one aspect of their multifaceted nature. Additionally, not every mythical narrative acts as a charter for cultural mores; rather, some myths are critical, and they question traditional values. As is discussed throughout this dissertation, superhero narratives can function to reinforce cultural values or they can question certain cultural institutions and assumptions. In general, it appears that the more typical superhero narratives tend to support traditionally held cultural values, but the more insightful and reflective superhero narratives, such as Alan Moore's *Watchmen* or Frank Miller's *The Dark Knight Returns*, tend to stand out as more critical of established cultural assumptions. It is not a contradiction that myths may either uphold or challenge cultural norms; rather, it furthers the premise that these narratives are subtly persuasive forces within society.

The founding premise of my research is that contemporary superhero narratives are modern myths in North American popular culture. Since the majority of superhero narratives find their roots in comic books, the structure of this dissertation will reflect the history of superheroes as they evolved in association with comics, periods such as the Golden Age of Superheroes, along with the Silver and Bronze Ages. Each of these Ages demarcates a certain era of superhero history, and the distinction between eras helps facilitate an appreciation of the growth of the superhero narrative. In line with this, the Golden section of this dissertation reflects its namesake Age of Superheroes by providing a historical foundation for the analysis that follows. Here, the Golden section is an overview of the history of the superhero from the 1938 initial publication of Superman in *Action Comics* to the present Marvel Comics' *Civil War*. This section explores the superhero's explosion into North American popular culture and how the superhero character has evolved over the decades. These first chapters place my own research into its historical context and they provide an overview of the complexities involved in the

17

superhero narrative's evolution. The Silver section follows, and it reflects the growth in the superhero narrative by adding theories of cultural analysis. The Silver section develops a semiotic analysis of prominent superheroes and their functions as cultural signs. This section will use the semiotic theories of Ferdinand de Saussure, Roland Barthes, and Umberto Eco in an analysis of the superhero as portrayed in comics, television, and film. In addition, Fredric Wertham's role in the backlash against the comics medium during the 1940s and 50s is also analyzed in the context of cultural analysis. Effectively, these chapters establish how superheroes hold significance within a culture and how they naturalize a culture's value systems. Ultimately, the Bronze section of my dissertation reflects upon the superhero narrative as it stands in the current Age of Superheroes. The Bronze section combines previously examined cultural theories with Fredric Jameson's ideas on utopia, in order to establish the superhero tale's function in contemporary North American popular culture while providing insight into the current state of North American popular values. The chapters in this section focus analyses on more contemporary superhero narratives that deal with increasingly complex issues, such as Alan Moore's *Watchmen* and Mark Millar's *Civil War*. By extrapolation, the influence of the superhero tale in North American culture can be taken as a case study of media's persuasive influence within a culture on a larger scale to include other forms of entertainment, advertising, propaganda, and journalism. With the three sections of my dissertation taken together, the cultural function of the superhero narrative becomes readily apparent. Likewise, I hope that the arguments presented here suggest that the cultural influence of other popular narratives should be brought under a microscope and subject to critical reflection.

18

GOLDEN

Origin Stories – The Superhero's History

A Brief History of Superheroes

And

Superheroes and the World War II Propaganda Monologue

A Brief History of Superheroes

The history of superheroes has traditionally been confused with the history of comics. Although superheroes and comics share many elements of the same history, too often the closeness of the two subjects has sparked confusion. Here, I focus on the history of the superhero and attempt to separate its history from some of the elements in the history of comics which are mistakenly included in the history of superheroes. There are three distinct paradigms in the history of the superhero genre, which is not accurately represented in any histories of comic books; however, by discerning content from the history of comics that is particularly relevant to superheroes and not necessarily industry-related, we can more accurately recount the history of the superhero genre.

The terminology used in the history of comics and superheroes has contributed to the problem of confusing the historical subjects. Traditionally, fans, collectors, academics, and historians refer to the Golden, Silver, and Bronze Ages of Comics. However, when they speak of the various ages, they may either be speaking of the state of the comics industry at that time, or the group of superheroes that are popular during that age, or they are speaking of both. There is some debate about how to demarcate the different ages, but Gemstone Publishing, the publisher of the authoritative *Overstreet Comic Book Price Guide*, proposes the following model (Rhoades 5):

TIME PERIOD	COMICS AGE	CATALYST
1828 – 82	Victorian Age	
1883 – 38	Platinum Age	
1938 – 45	Golden Age	*Action Comics* #1
1946 – 56	Atomic Age	Fear of Bomb

1956 – 71	Silver Age	*Showcase* #4
1971 – 85	Bronze Age	Death of Gwen Stacy (*AMZ* #121)
1986 – 92	Copper Age	DC's *Crisis*
1992 – 99	Chrome Age	Image Comics debuts
2000 – Present	Modern Age	

The above table is representative of the standard timeline for discussing the history of comics and superheroes. With regards to the history of comics, this historical breakdown may suffice, but it falls short of helpful when considering the history of superheroes. In the history of modern superheroes, there are three distinct paradigms with clearly corresponding catalytic events. Thus, I propose the following categorization for the history of superheroes:

TIME PERIOD	SUPERHERO AGE	CATALYST
1938 – 61	Golden Age	*Action Comics* #1
1961 – 86	Silver Age	*Fantastic Four* #1; Spider-Man
1986 – Present	Bronze Age	*Watchmen*; *Dark Knight Returns*

Although each catalyst which triggers a paradigm shift in the history of superheroes is rooted in comic book publications, the trend is developed across superheroes in various media. The remainder of this essay argues for this structure as the more accurate, efficient, and useful categorization of the history of superheroes.

The argument that the development of the superhero must be viewed as three progressing cultural paradigms requires a brief explanation of Ludwig Wittgenstein's idea of a language game and Thomas Kuhn's notions of paradigms and incommensurability. Wittgenstein introduced the "language game" as a means of understanding the meaning of words in the philosophy of language. Basically, a language game is the context within which a word finds meaning (Wittgenstein S7, S47, S65). If one were to ask a question that has no specified language game (or comes from one language game inquiring of another), then one cannot expect to understand or appreciate the answer (Wittgenstein S47). Kuhn's "paradigm" is rooted in Wittgenstein's language game; however, Kuhn intended for the paradigm to apply specifically to the scientific community. For Kuhn, a paradigm "[characterizes] a scientific tradition, including its theory, textbook problems and solutions, its apparatus, methodology, and its philosophy of science" (Rosenberg 178). Kuhn's "incommensurability" is, essentially, "the supposed untranslatability of one theory or paradigm into another... [and] in moving from one [paradigm] to another, there will be explanatory losses as well as gains" (Rosenberg 177). In addition, notice that paradigm shifts do occur as the result of making the leap from one paradigm to another. In Kuhn's sense of scientific paradigms, consider when Einstein advances scientific theory beyond Newtonian physics. This is not so much bridging the gap of incommensurability, but moreso the usurping of a paradigm. While Wittgenstein uses the language game approach to understand language, and Kuhn uses the paradigm to understand scientific eras, the approach is effective in understanding cultures as well. I adopt a Kuhnian approach to the terminology, labelling our social contexts cultural paradigms. By doing so, I hope to invoke the stronger sense of a collection of beliefs, attitudes, and ideas implied by the term "paradigm," as opposed to the loose connotation of a simpler "social context."

The Golden Age of Superheroes begins with their introduction en masse to North American popular culture. The most popular superhero characters of that period persist today in popular culture, such as Superman, Batman, Wonder Woman, and Captain America. Shirrel Rhoades explains in *A Complete History of American Comics* that, little suspecting it would become the most successful comic book property ever created, DC Comics' editor, Vin Sullivan, included Superman in the June 1938 publication *Action Comics* #1, despite having previously rejected the idea as a comic strip (Rhoades 17). According to Danny Fingeroth in *Disguised as Clark Kent*, Joe Shuster and Jerry Siegel had become dependable freelancers for DC Comics[2], and pitched the idea of a Superman comic strip several times, only to be rejected; however, when DC was putting together a new title, *Action Comics*, the publisher was desperate for material to fill the comic book, and Siegel and Shuster's success as freelancers helped pave the way for Superman's inclusion in the book (Fingeroth 40-41). The first Superman story published in *Action Comics* #1 in 1938 was hastily compiled from the artists' demo strips into a single continuity (Fingeroth 42). As such, *Action Comics* #1 is the catalyst for the Golden Age of Superheroes, since it is the first appearance of Superman in any media, and Superman was the driving force behind the initial success of the superhero genre. As the story goes, Superman is the last survivor of the planet Krypton, sent to earth as an infant. As a Kryptonian on Earth, Superman is gifted with an array of superpowers ranging from superstrength to x-ray vision. Raised by the Kents on a farm in Smallville, Superman was brought up to be honest and just. Not long after his creation, Superman had transcended comics, entering various other forms of popular media. Fingeroth explains this further in the following passage:

[2] Both DC Comics and Marvel Comics were known by different company names throughout the ages before settling on their current identities. DC was once known as national Comics, and Marvel previously known as Timely Comics and also as Atlas Comics. To avoid confusion, I will refer to the companies only as Marvel or DC.

> Superman also signalled the arrival of comic books as a spawning ground for characters that crossed media boundaries. Within a very short time of his first appearance in comics, Superman was featured in movie serials, on the radio, in cartoons, and, coming full circle, in a newspaper comic strip produced by Siegel and Shuster. (Fingeroth 42)

Superman's adventures also transformed comic books into a mass medium which, in turn, spawned a legion of other superheroes from DC Comics and the competition (Fingeroth 42).

There were three other major superhero characters that helped shape the Golden Age of Superheroes – Batman, Captain America, and Wonder Woman. According to Ron Goulart in *The Comic Book Encyclopedia*, Batman was created by Bob Kane and Bill Finger[3] immediately following the success of Superman, and he first appears in *Detective Comics* #27, May 1939 (Goulart 34). While Batman has no superhuman powers or abilities, "he [has] trained himself in body and mind to the peak of human perfectibility" (Fingeroth 55). For readers who found Superman's abilities too farfetched, or just as a contrast, Batman was the alternative (Fingeroth 55). The founding premise of the Batman story is that he witnessed the murder of his millionaire parents as a young child, and swore an oath to dedicate his life to fighting crime. Thus, he pursued extensive physical training and intellectual education. In his battles against criminals and villains, he utilizes a vast array of gadgetry in fighting crime, such as his batbelt, batarangs, and the batmobile.

In 1940, at what would later become Marvel Comics, Martin Goodman asked Jack Kirby and Joe Simon to come up with a superhero character to compete with the Shield, a patriotic hero who was appearing in MLJ's popular *Pep Comics* (Rhoades 33).[4]

---

[3] Finger rarely receives any official credit for co-creating Batman, although it was a collaborative effort (Goulart 34).
[4] MLJ Comics has little to do with superheroes after the Golden Age. However, it built its success on a comedic character named Archie, and later renamed itself Archie Comics.

So Simon and Kirby created a red-white-and-blue superhero character that embodied the quintessence of patriotism, Captain America (Rhoades 33). In an unusual move, Goodman introduced the character in his own title, and *Captain America Comics* #1 displayed Captain America on the cover punching Hitler in the face (Rhoades 33). Fingeroth explains the Captain America's origin story as follows:

> Captain America started out as Steve Rogers, a poor, scrawny kid who wanted to join the United States Army to fight Hitler – well before Pearl Harbor – but was rejected 4-F, unfit for duty because of his frail physical condition. He volunteered to take part in the "Project: Super Soldier" experiments led by Professor Reinstein – a thinly disguised homage to Albert Einstein – and emerged from the procedure as the peak-of-human-perfection Captain America. (Fingeroth 58)

Captain America was tremendously successful, at times outselling even the Superman and Batman comics (Fingeroth 57).

The final major superhero introduced during the Golden Age of Superheroes turned out to be a superheroine. Marc Edward DiPaolo explains in "Wonder Woman as World War II Veteran, Camp Feminist Icon, and Male Sex Fantasy" that William Moulton Marston created Wonder Woman for DC Comics in 1941, and she debuted in *All Star Comics* #8 (DiPaolo 151-152). Marston was a psychologist and a student of the psychological effects of mass media on the individual spectator, an advocate of the reformation of criminals, and an early developer of the lie-detector test (DiPaolo 152). DiPaolo further explains that "Marston created the comic book character Wonder Woman to be both strong and sexy as a means of encouraging women to emulate her unapologetic assertiveness" (DiPaolo 153). Based loosely on Greek myth, Wonder Woman is an Amazon princess, hailing from Themiscyra, also known as Paradise Island. The Amazons have been blessed by the goddess Aphrodite, and they are gifted with eternal life, superior strength, and access to advanced technologies (DiPaolo 153). During World

War II, Wonder Woman acted almost as an Amazonian ambassador, fighting Axis spies and terrorists on the American homefront, promoting women's equality, and preaching about the peace to come (DiPaolo 154).

Together, these four major characters of the Golden Age of Superheroes helped solidify the foundation and tropes of the superhero genre. As a paradigm, the Golden Age of Superheroes set forth some of the most recognizable superhero tropes. Superheroes were defined as costumed crimefighters and do-gooders, many of which had superpowers, like Superman and Wonder Woman, while a few had little to no special powers, like Batman and Captain America. These superheroes generally had secret identities, and they fought criminals and villains. In Scott Zakarian's "Here Come the Heroes," Stan Lee remembers the comic book industry of Golden Age as follows:

> Comic books always [in the early years] followed trends – for a couple of years it would be superheroes, then it would be romance, or westerns, or animated [comedic] characters. And, we were real followers. Whatever the trend was, we would put out a lot of books in that trend... and I went along with him [the publisher, Martin Goodman], whatever had to be written, I wrote. ("Here Come the Heroes" 00:05:00)

Accordingly, the superhero genre did not dominate the comics medium for the entire duration of what I have termed the Golden Age of Superheroes. Amy Kiste Nyberg maintains in *Seal of Approval: The History of the Comics Code* that the public had largely lost interest in superhero comics shortly after the war, and the dominant genre of comic books shifted towards the crime and horror stories (Nyberg 17). Traditionally, the Golden Age of Comics is marked as ending with the crusade against comics and Fredric Wertham's biased criticism of the comic book medium, *Seduction of the Innocent*, in 1954 (Rhoades 58).[5] However, it is important to recognize that although the comic book industry suffered in sales around this time and the dominant genres shifted from

---

[5] The crusade against comics and, in particular, Fredric Wertham's critique of comic books is the subject of a later chapter, "The Superhero Narrative's Influence on its Audience."

superheroes, this is not a sufficient reason to signify an end to the Golden Age of Superheroes. In *Super Heroes: A Modern Mythology*, Richard Reynolds notes that "the Big Three," Superman, Batman and Wonder Woman, have continuously remained in print since their creation (Reynolds 7). The crucial factor here is that the superhero paradigm remained the same throughout the period where the comic book industry endured poor sales and furious criticism.

Some historians claim the Silver Age of Comics began in 1956 when the superhero genre makes a triumphant return to the comic book industry thanks to DC's editor in chief Julius Schwartz (Rhoades 70). This is also evident in Gemstone Publishing's time table presented above, which notes DC Comics' *Showcase* #4 as the catalytic event of the Silver Age of Comics. Under Schwartz's direction, writer Gardner Fox and artist Carmine Infantino re-created The Flash for publication in *Showcase* #4, and, following this success, DC's line expanded with new versions of Green Lantern, Hawkman, and many others, while also reintroducing the superhero team once known as the Justice Society of America as the Justice League of America (Rhoades 70). However, this initial resurgence of superheroes in the marketplace is not sufficient to be recognized as the catalytic event triggering the Silver Age of Superheroes, even if it is a significant event in the history of comic books. This second wave of superheroes from DC delivered stories in the same vein as the Golden Age of Superheroes. As such, in my proposed time table presented above, the Golden Age of Superheroes reaches from 1938, endures the poor sales and criticism of the 1950s, and includes the reintroduction of DC's superheroes. The superhero paradigm does not progress until Marvel Comics allows Stan

Lee to create a new wave of superheroes to compete with DC's renewed success in the genre.

Since public interest in superheroes returns with DC Comics' second wave of superhero tales – combined with the success of television's *The Adventures of Superman*, featuring George Reeves – other publishers felt secure experimenting with the superhero genre again (Rhoades 71). In 1961 Stan Lee and Jack Kirby created *The Fantastic Four* #1, a team of superheroes with human failings and fears, the likes of which was a sharp departure from "the unblemished do-gooder archetypes" of previously established superheroes (Rhoades 78). Stan Lee's legacy is, essentially, the defining factor of the Silver Age of Superheroes. Not long after creating the Fantastic Four, Lee published another groundbreaking superhero, Spider-Man. Similar to the circumstances surrounding Superman's creation, when Lee first proposed a Spider-Man comic to his editor, the response was that people hate spiders, teenagers are only suitable for sidekick characters, and no one wanted to read a book where the hero has realistic problems, like problems with money and girls ("Creating Spider-Man" 00:01:45). One Marvel series that Lee had been working on, *Amazing Fantasy*, was about to be cancelled, and Lee decided to take a risk and publish the first Spider-Man story in its final issue ("Creating Spider-Man" 00:04:10). After August 1962, when Spider-Man was introduced in *Amazing Fantasy* #15, he quickly became Marvel's best-selling character (Rhoades 81). The story of Spider-Man begins when a teenager, Peter Parker, is bitten by a radioactive spider. This imbues Parker with the proportional strength of a spider, the ability to stick to smooth surfaces, and, thanks to his own scientific ingenuity, he also develops wrist-mounted web shooters. Parker's first instinct is to use his new powers for his own personal, financial gain, but when he fails to act in the course of a robbery, it results in his Uncle Ben's murder. This tragedy is Parker's impetus for becoming the superhero Spider-Man. In Zakarian's "Creating Spider-Man," Lee acknowledges that the character's tremendous success was largely due to the fact that Peter Parker was more relatable to his mostly teenage readership than other superheroes at the time ("Creating Spider-Man" 00:06:10). With Lee as its guiding force, Marvel Comics re-entered the superhero market with a slew of successful new characters, such as the Fantastic Four, the Hulk, Spider-Man, the X-Men, Thor, and Iron Man, additionally reintroducing Golden Age characters such as Captain America (Reynolds 9). Lee's Marvel superheroes really usher in the Silver Age of Superheroes. This new notion of heroes with human failings begins with *Fantastic Four* #1 and is epitomized with Spider-Man.

However, besides introducing superhero characters with human failings, Lee developed a storytelling technique hitherto unused in superhero comics – he presented stories as serials with continuity. Prior to *Fantastic Four* #1, superhero stories had generally been self-contained; however, Lee and his collaborators created stories that "not only continued directly from one issue to the next – with subplots and cliffhangers – of a specific title but, with increasing regularity, spilled over into the events of other series" (Rhoades 80). This brought superhero stories from a series of unconnected, episodic adventures into the realm of a connected and overlapping continuity of superhero narratives. Today, superhero continuity like this is a mainstay of the genre, not only in comics but in television series and movies, as well. At the time this change was both radical and popular, making Marvel a dominant force during the Silver Age, while DC struggled since they were so slow adopting the new style (Rhoades 80).

29

Nevertheless, each of the major superhero publishing houses adopted this new style, thus bringing about the Marvel Universe and DC Universe of characters which was rich with mythos and a complex, sometimes contradictory, continuity. Accordingly, the Silver Age of Superheroes is characterized by superheroes with human failings and serialized storytelling, which we can largely credit to Stan Lee.

Following the Golden and Silver Ages of Superheroes is where my timeline most drastically departs from the traditional Comic Book Ages. The Gemstone Publishing timeline of Comic Book Ages posits a Bronze Age of Comics from 1971 – 1985 which is allegedly instigated by the death of Gwen Stacy in *Amazing Spider-Man* #121. Gwen Stacy was Peter Parker's love interest, who died accidentally when Spider-Man tried to rescue her from a sadistic trap set by the Green Goblin. This appears to be an almost arbitrary historical marker for the comic book industry. Furthermore, while it may be a significant event in Spider-Man cannon, it does not signify a paradigm shift in the superhero genre. The death of Gwen Stacy did not send out changes that rippled through superhero storytelling. Rather, this event seems to be a product of Stan Lee's legacy of superheroes dealing with more human problems, albeit a much more tragic problem for the protagonist than impressing his friends or paying the rent. Additionally, Gemstone posits a Copper Age of Comics spanning from 1986 – 1992, which is triggered by DC Comics' *Crisis on Infinite Earths*. Again, this comes across as an arbitrary marker for comic book history. DC's *Crisis* was merely the company's attempt to reboot their primary superhero characters and alleviate them from a hefty, convoluted, and sometimes contradictory continuity. Essentially, this DC storyline was meant to clean up the mess they had made with their characters since 1938. While cleaning up the DC cannon was a massive task, it did not offer anything to change the superhero dynamic in any substantial way. Gemstone then posits a Chrome Age of Comics from 1992 – 1999, apparently instigated by the creation of Image Comics. Granted, the comics industry was undergoing some changes around this period in time. For instance, Image Comics and Dark Horse Comics both emerge and stake a substantial claim on the market. However, these events represent changes in the comic book industry and marketplace, not in the way in which superhero tales were told. Hence, when considering the history of superheroes, I propose rejecting the Gemstone designations for the Bronze, Copper, Chrome, and Modern Ages (which Gemstone has left unqualified with regards to its catalytic event), since these clearly do not reflect any change in the superhero paradigm.

Instead, the Bronze Age of Superheroes must reflect a profound change in the superhero paradigm. This revolution occurs nearly simultaneously in 1986 when DC Comics publishes Frank Miller's *The Dark Knight Returns* and Alan Moore's *Watchmen*. In "Superhero Revisionism in *Watchmen* and *The Dark Knight Returns*," Aeon J. Skoble explains their influence as follows:

> These two graphic novels have been enormously influential in terms of how superheroes have been presented and thought of since the mid-to-late 1980s. Many sophisticated elements of comics today that we now take as givens – the way they raise questions of justice and vengeance, their exploration of the ethics of vigilantism, and their depiction of ambivalent and even hostile reactions towards superheroes from the general public as well as from government – are largely traceable to these works. (Skoble 29)

These two titles deconstructed the superhero genre so thoroughly that for several years any superhero comic that continued in the traditional vein of storytelling seemed like nothing more than a bad parody of the superhero genre (Rhoades 125).

Miller's *The Dark Knight Returns* explicitly examines the moral issues surrounding superhero vigilantism as it portrays the Batman's psyche as much more deeply traumatized by his parents' murder than it had been previously portrayed (Skoble 31). The premise of *The Dark Knight Returns* is that "Batman had once enjoyed a close relationship with the police, but was obliged to 'retire' after public anti-vigilante pressure, and when he returns a decade later, he soon finds a new police commissioner issuing a warrant for his arrest" (Skoble 31). Superman also appears in the story and, in contrast to Batman, Miller has Superman respond to the same pressures that mount against freely operating vigilantes by becoming a secret agent of the government (Skoble 32). Batman regards Superman as submitting to government pressure and coercion, but Superman sees his work for the government as justified in utilitarian terms, as directed towards a greater good (Skoble 32). Skoble explains Batman's position as follows:

> For Batman, the presence of a badge or a flag is neither necessary nor sufficient for justice. Laws may be unjust, politicians may be corrupt, and the legal system may actually protect the wicked, but none of this will deter Batman from his mission. (Skoble 32)

This is interesting since it challenges the reader to think ethically about the nature of superheroism, vigilante crime-fighting, and the relationship between what is just and what is legal.

Moore's *Watchmen* is groundbreaking along similar grounds since it also challenges readers to consider the nature of the superhero. Skoble summarizes the incredibly rich and intricate *Watchmen* as follows:

> Moore creates an entirely new and different collection of masked crime-fighters, along with one clearly superhuman superhero. The world of Moore's story begins by asking the question of what would happen if the 1938 release of the first "Superman" comic book story had inspired some real people to become masked crime-fighters. He then recapitulates the comic book history by inventing a "golden age" collection of superheroes and various costumed vigilantes, as well as a later generation following in their footsteps. The narrative of *Watchmen* uses them to delve into the psychology as well as the ethical and political ramifications of vigilantism. (Skoble 34)

Moore has developed a thoroughly detailed background or a self-contained continuity to serve as the world in which his superheroes exist. Furthermore, Moore's characters operate with multiple layers of pastiche. For instance, Nite Owl is lifted from Blue Beetle, who in turn has been cloned from Batman. Accordingly, the characters in *Watchmen* speak to the audience as indirect representations of familiar superhero archetypes. Since *Watchmen* was published by DC Comics, this allowed Moore to freely work with obvious clones of major DC Comics characters, while simultaneously maintaining complete distance from directly affecting those characters' continuity. Moore's narrative operates on many complex levels, commenting on everything from the absurdities of the superhero genre to sexuality and gender.

Taken together, *The Dark Knight Returns* and *Watchmen* constitute the catalytic event shifting the superhero paradigm into the Bronze Age of Superheroes. These are two of the three texts which are generally regarded to have brought a sense of maturity to the medium, garnering academic and literary attention.[6] In the case of Frank Miller's graphic novel, *The Dark Knight Returns*, Will Brooker argues in "The Best Batman Story: *The Dark Knight Returns*" that it has tremendous importance for both comic books in general and the Batman mythos, with effects that influence comics and films nearly 20 years after the work's initial release. For instance, the importance of *The Dark Knight Returns* has trickled down to recognition of more obscure works in comics (Brooker 41-42), and it inspired the darker, grimmer atmospheres of Batman movies by Tim Burton in 1989 and Christopher Nolan in 2005 (Brooker 43). Likewise, *Watchmen* has certainly influenced later superhero narratives such as Brad Meltzer's *Identity Crisis*, Mark

---

[6] The third revolutionary graphic novel is Art Spiegelman's *Maus*. However, since it is not a superhero narrative, it does not warrant significant attention here.

Millar's *Civil War*, and Bruce Timm and Paul Dini's cartoon series, *Justice League Unlimited*. Additionally, a *Watchmen* film is scheduled to release in theatres in early 2009. In the Bronze Age of Superheroes, what was once a safe and juvenile realm of fiction has given way to something far more relevant. The genre has become much less about fanciful escapism; instead, the new superhero paradigm allows the reader to examine issues which bear significance on the real world. The Bronze Age of Superheroes is reflective upon what it means to be a superhero or vigilante. This new paradigm even trickles down into the more commercialized comic book series of Marvel and DC to an extent that was hitherto nonexistent prior to *Watchmen* and *The Dark Knight Returns*.

Considering the aforementioned arguments, there are three distinct paradigms in the history of the superhero genre. Thus, the following categorization for the history of superheroes is fair and accurate:

TIME PERIOD	SUPERHERO AGE	CATALYST
1938 – 61	Golden Age	*Action Comics* #1
1961 – 86	Silver Age	*Fantastic Four* #1; Spider-Man
1986 – Present	Bronze Age	*Watchmen*; *Dark Knight Returns*

Although the history of the superhero genre is closely tied to the history of comic books, they exhibit unique, defining characteristics that differentiate their histories. The Golden Age of Superheroes begins with their introduction into popular culture. The Golden Age of Superheroes helped solidify the foundation and tropes of the superhero genre. Superheroes were characterized as costumed crimefighters and do-gooders adventurers. Typically, these superheroes had secret identities, and used their alternate superhero personae to fight crime. Stan Lee's superheroes, produced for Marvel, usher in the Silver Age of Superheroes. His superheroes demonstrated human failings, beginning with *Fantastic Four* #1 and epitomized with Spider-Man. Additionally, the Silver Age of Superheroes is characterized by Lee's storytelling technique which presented stories as serials with continuity. The Bronze Age of Superheroes revolutionizes the superhero paradigm by reflecting upon what it means to be a superhero or vigilante. Miller and Moore deconstructed the established tropes of the superhero genre, challenging readers to confront the issues surrounding justice and vigilantism. This more mature mode of storytelling has since permeated the superhero genre across various media, thus defining the Bronze Age of Superheroes. As such, this constitutes a history of the superhero which is distinct from the history of the comic book medium.

Superheroes and the World War II Propaganda Monologue

Danny Fingeroth writes in *Superman on the Couch* that "the superhero has evolved in collective consciousness to the point where it may not even matter where the concept originally came from" (Fingeroth 45). While Fingeroth is correct to acknowledge the pervasiveness of the superhero figure in North American popular culture, he is flippant to dismiss the importance of understanding the modern superhero's cultural roots. Instead, researching the origins of the modern superhero will both develop a more comprehensive picture of North American culture surrounding World War II and facilitate a more thorough understanding of the function of the superhero figure in popular narratives. As such, after considering Friedrich Nietzsche's historiography, I interrogate the superhero's emergence into mainstream popular culture during the American war effort by focusing on Superman and Batman's close knit relationship to the propaganda monologue of World War II.

Certain historiographers would not likely attribute much value in researching the historical origin of the modern superhero. Yet, if the superhero is considered as a modern myth, then the value of its analysis becomes more evident. The superhero is not merely a cliché of popular culture; rather, the superhero has been a central figure in North America's modern myths since their inception. Here, myth refers not simply to a falsehood, but to narrative tales which "function to express social values, norms of behaviour, and/or the consequences of deviating from them" (Harris & Platzner 13). Although many myths are set in the remote past, this is not necessary for a narrative to function as a significant myth within a culture, hence superhero tales of the past hundred years count as modern myths. The most significant difference between a historical

36

narrative and a mythical narrative is that history is held to a high standard of factual truth, while myth requires little to no foundation in facts.

Friedrich Nietzsche's historiography is one such philosophy of history that emphasizes the importance of understanding a culture's myths. Considering Nietzsche's arguments, the determination of factual truth in history and myth is less important than understanding the cultural values that are expressed in their narratives. In "Myth is Higher than History," Nietzsche holds that "the state itself has no unwritten laws more powerful than the mythical foundation that guarantees... its growth out of mythical representations" (Nietzsche 150). Hugh Rayment-Pickard explains in *Philosophies of History* that Nietzsche is primarily concerned with the values expressed through histories and myths because he considers facts to be, essentially, value judgements (Rayment-Pickard 139). Since the group's collective beliefs determine what is taken to be true in a culture, then both history and myth share a strong similarity in that they are both propagated by a culture's values. Accordingly, Nietzsche upholds mythical analyses as more important than historical analyses, since myths are narratives tailored to express social values. Therefore, in researching the origin of North America's modern superhero, I am primarily concerned with the values represented in the early superhero tales of the World War II era.

The history of the modern superhero truly begins when Superman and Batman emerge into comic books and quickly dominate the market. Superman debuted in *Action Comics* #1 in 1938 and was followed by Batman in *Detective Comics* #27 in 1939; both characters proving to be immediate hits amongst comic book readers (Fingeroth 44). The success of Superman and Batman led to the competition's creation of their own

37

superheroes. In "American Dreams of Mutants," John M. Trushell explains that this superhero boom established the comics' "golden age," introducing Marvel Comics' characters such as The Human Torch,[7] Namor the Sub-Mariner, and Captain America (Trushell 150). Superhero comics, in particular, "flourished for the golden age before and during the Second World War" (Trushell 151). Amy Kiste Nyberg maintains in *Seal of Approval: The History of the Comics Code* that shortly after World War II, the public had largely lost interest in super hero comics, and the dominant genre of comic books shifted towards the crime and horror stories of pulp fiction (Nyberg 17). This shift brought previously mild criticism to a furious zenith (Nyberg 17). The crusade against comics, which followed in the post-war era, is dominated by the criticism of Dr. Fredric Wertham, psychiatrist and expert on juvenile delinquency, and by the introduction of the comics code, the comic book publishers' means of self-censorship. The Golden Age of Comics ended in 1954 with Frederic Wertham's lengthy book, *Seduction of the Innocent* (Trushell 151), which argues that there is a correlative link between juvenile delinquency and reading comic books.

However, it should be made clear that the comic book readership was made up of more than just juvenile boys. Rather, in "Comic Books During World War II: Defending the American Way of Life," Ian Gordon reports that, by 1944, "41 percent of men between the ages of eighteen and thirty read comic books regularly, which researchers defined as more than six comic books a month" (Gordon 70). In addition, Gordon writes that 28 percent of women between age eighteen and thirty regularly read comic books in 1944 (Gordon 70). He further maintains that between 1941 and 1944 comic books sales

---

[7] Note that this is not the Human Torch of the Fantastic Four. The original Human Torch was an android engulfed in flames.

had doubled from ten million to twenty million copies sold each month (Gordon 70). With such large numbers of adults reading comic books, it is a blatant misrepresentation of the medium to categorize comic books merely as children's literature. Gordon also suggests that military service during this period "led to increased comic book readership" (Gordon 71). In support of this claim Gordon cites the fact that comic book sales in overseas post exchanges "outsold the combined circulation of *Reader's Digest*, *Life*, and *The Saturday Evening Post*" (Gordon 71). Undoubtedly, the Second World War significantly affected the pervasiveness of the superhero figure, but it had a profound influence on the content of superhero narratives, as well.

The modern superhero figure was still in its infancy when America joined the war effort. Some publishers at the time had their superhero characters confront the Axis both at home and overseas. The superhero figures in many publications, such as Marvel's, dealt with warfare in a direct and hands-on manner; however, the narratives of both Superman and Batman largely avoided any direct confrontation with the conflicts overseas. As Will Brooker characterizes the wartime era in *Batman Unmasked*, "Virtually every form of popular culture was co-opted into a wartime propaganda monologue, with the shared agenda of presenting a unified front to the consumer public" (Brooker 67). Superman and Batman are no exception to this, yet historians such as Gordon and Brooker dispute the extent to which these superheroes' narratives are propagandized. Although Superman and Batman may not often directly confront the Axis in their stories, both characters maintain a tight relationship with World War II, one that essentially shapes how their respective mythoi develop over the following decades.

Before interrogating how World War II helped define two of the world's most recognizable superheroes, one must consider the history of the creation of these characters. Bob Hughes writes in the introduction to *Superman in the Forties* that Superman is originally a product of the mid-thirties, created by Jerry Siegel and Joe Shuster, inspired by pulp representations of Zorro, Tarzan, and Robin Hood, and initially an unsuccessful comic strip (*Superman in the Forties* 5). Siegel and Shuster's Superman would not be published until a new publisher took the reins of Detective Comics, and set out to launch a new comic book magazine, titled *Action Comics* (*Superman in the Forties* 5). According to Hughes, Donenfeld gave the creators merely a few days to reformat the Superman daily comic strips into a comic book layout, and "in April 1938, the first issue of *Action Comics* hit the stands with Siegel and Shuster's Superman on the cover, lifting an automobile over his head and scaring the bejeezus out of everyone in sight" (*Superman in the Forties* 5-6).[8] While the publisher may have been apprehensive about the first issue of *Action Comics*, Superman went on to become a quick success, appearing in daily newspapers, making a "personal appearance" at the World's Fair, receiving his own comic book, and a radio show within a few short months from his initial publication (*Superman in the Forties* 6). According to Ron Goulart in *The Comic Book Encyclopedia*, Superman single-handedly "turned the fledgling comic book business into a major industry, changing the look and content of the four-color magazines forever" (Goulart 320). While it may be surprising to those familiar with Superman's modern mythos, Hughes describes the early Superman not as a crime fighter but a "wisecracking, whirling dervish of energy, popping out of the sky to right a wrong, stop a bully, save a child or frighten an unscrupulous businessman into giving someone a fair deal"

---

[8] See Figure 1 for the cover of *Action Comics* #1.

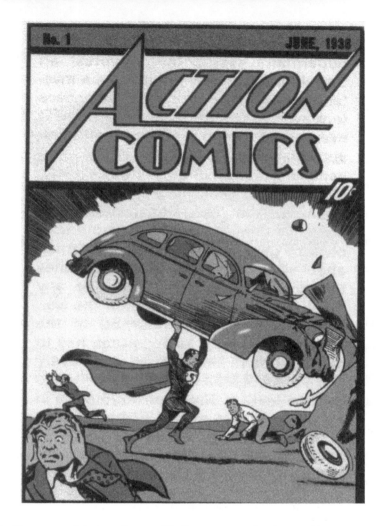

Figure 1: The cover of Action Comics #1 (Superman in the Forties 8).

(*Superman in the Forties* 6). Following such acts of heroism, Superman would "[disappear] into the night, accompanied by a hail of police bullets" (*Superman in the Forties* 6). In addition, Hughes maintains that in Superman's earliest adventures "whenever he vanished, some poor Joe's life was better off, and some rich SOB had had his pockets picked" (*Superman in the Forties* 6). To his Depression-weary readership in 1938, Superman was the hero of the underprivileged working class, a decidedly Marxist hero for the proletariat. However, this form of Marxist heroism would not last long as part of the Superman mythos, and when America enters World War II Superman's ideology takes a swift turn to consumerism.

Nevertheless, in order to facilitate a better appreciation of Superman's ideological shift, we must first consider Batman's relationship with the war effort. Goulart explains that Batman is created by Bob Kane and Bill Finger following the success of Superman, and he first appears in *Detective Comics* #27, May 1939 (Goulart 34).[9] Like Superman, Batman, too, was inspired by pulp characters, such as the Shadow and the Spider (Goulart 35). In April 1940, Batman received a sidekick, Robin, and he also warranted his own bi-monthly, spin-off comic book, *Batman*, first published in April-May 1940 (Brooker 34). Brooker summarizes Batman's character as follows:

> Batman is Bruce Wayne, a millionaire who dresses in a bat-costume and fights crime. He has no special powers but is very fit and strong, and very intelligent. He lives in Gotham City. He fights crime because his parents were killed when he was young. He is often helped by his sidekick, Robin. He fights villains like the Joker. (Brooker 40)

Brooker argues that these essential elements of Batman's character originate in his early narratives and remain largely immune to the "propaganda monologue" of World War II (Brooker 35). However, the perseverance of Batman's essential characteristics

---

[9] See Figure 2 for the cover of *Detective Comics* #27.

Figure 2: The cover of Detective Comics #27 (Batman in the Forties 8).

throughout the decades does not entail that the Batman narratives were immune to the propaganda monologue during the war.

Considering Gordon's arguments in contrast to Brooker's, it is apparent that the Batman narratives during World War II played a significant role as propaganda, and the nature of their role will shed light on the ideological shift of the Superman narratives of that era. Brooker maintains that "there are propaganda messages within Batman comics of the war years but these are almost entirely along the lines of war bonds appeals rather than militaristic or anti-Japanese content" (Brooker 35). Furthermore, he asserts that the vast majority of these appeals are restricted to cover images (Brooker 35), later reiterating that "there is a marked distinction between a patriotic cover and a patriotic content" (Brooker 74). To a certain extent, Brooker's argument has a sound basis in fact; he supports his claims by citing that "eleven patriotic covers from all three titles [*Detective Comics*, *Batman*, and *World's Finest*] is not a significant proportion from a grand total of eighty-eight" (Brooker 74). Although Brooker concedes that, of the three Batman titles, there are four stories which can be loosely regarded as war-related (Brooker 76-77), he maintains that these stories are insignificant compared to overtly patriotic comics, such as *Captain America Special*, which "shows Cap and his sidekick Bucky wading through a battlefield of enemy soldiers, dealing out uppercuts and shooting down attacking aircraft" (Brooker 77). Based upon a lack of direct contact with enemy forces, Brooker holds that Batman could not have played a significant role in the campaign to rally support for the war.

However, while Batman may not have been a blatant cheerleader for the war effort, he remains a significant contributor to the propaganda monologue insofar as he

44

consistently promoted supporting the war effort through consumerism. Brooker's criterion for participation in the propaganda campaign is superficial and insufficient. It is not enough to analyze how frequently a superhero confronts adversaries who clearly and visibly represent the Axis; rather, one ought to consider the war of ideologies at play during the Second World War, as well, and analyze how superhero narratives support the war effort through their heroic exploits in general. Accordingly, consider how Batman's typical adversaries illustrate the narrative's ideology. Brooker admits that Batman narratives of the war years "focus on petty crime and their stock cast of thugs and outlandishly costumed villains" (Brooker 74). While the Joker does appear early in Batman's mythos, in *Batman* #1 (Goulart 37), a major portion of his adversaries are common gangsters and thugs (Brooker 50), and these adversaries portray the narrative's ideological tendencies. By combating petty thieves, Batman was promoting responsible consumerism. Gordon writes that since 1939 the North American advertising industry "consciously depicted consumer choice as a constituent element in and guarantee of political democracy" (Gordon 75). By the 1940s, identifying advertising and consumption with American values had become the ideology of "the American Way" (Gordon 75). Responsible consumption was seen as a significant means of supporting the war abroad, and Gordon elaborates as follows, saying that:

> During the war the industry's War Advertising Council acted as a clearinghouse for both the government's and private industry's wartime propaganda. Much of this advertising addressed citizens as consumers, urging them to cut back on their consumption of goods and cooperate with government measures to increase war production. (Gordon 75)

It follows that superheroes fighting petty thieves and greedy criminals on the home front were also promoting hegemonic ideals of responsible consumerism to their readerships. Gordon argues that the content of Batman narratives bear a striking resemblance to these

45

propagandized advertisements (Gordon 76). He also notes that it is typical for general works on American culture between 1941 and 1945 to acknowledge the overt patriotism of characters such as Captain America, but dismiss the content of both Batman and Superman comics (Gordon 76). As such, Brooker's analysis of Batman's role in the war-time propaganda monologue is not unexpected. While Brooker provides an accurate account of overt support for the war in Batman narratives, Gordon provides a more convincing argument that the content of Batman narratives consistently portrays the rhetoric of the North American propaganda monologue of World War II. Gordon further explains that most war-era Batman stories "depicted a universe in which American soldiers fought to establish world peace while [Batman] helped to maintain a domestic order that supported the country's military endeavours "(Gordon 77). In this manner, Batman contributed to foster an ideological foundation of consumerism within his readership. Contrary to Brooker's account, Batman's essential characteristics remained consistent throughout the war-era only because they already conformed to the ideals of responsible consumerism.

However, in order for Superman to properly portray a unified home front of responsible consumers, he required an abrupt shift in his ideological tendencies. Brooker seems to adequately recognize this ideological shift in Superman, despite missing the significance of Batman's ideology in relation to the war. He explains that Superman was "put through subtle changes to tame his lawlessness and faintly radical edge, and transform him into a more unambiguously patriotic hero" (Brooker 65). Apparently, Brooker recognizes the significance of Superman's shift to a more consumerist ideology while failing to acknowledge the importance of Batman's own consumerist heroism.

46

Nevertheless, Superman noticeably shifts his ideology such that his adventures begin linking patriotism to legitimate business, while he consistently thwarts illicit business (Gordon 79). The original Superman of 1938, hero of the underprivileged working class, has given way to the new Superman of the war effort, supporting complacent consumerism and upholding the values of the capitalist, industrial empire.

During World War II, both Superman and Batman narratives functioned as charters for supporting the war effort, upholding the "American way" of consumerism. While consumption may not have been an explicit theme, Gordon asserts that "it formed the social backdrop in which stories were set" (Gordon 77). Additionally, he maintains that superhero tales, such as those of Superman and Batman, bind together the war effort, democracy, and consumer culture, and that these narratives demonstrate the close connection between democratic ideals and consumerism in North American culture (Gordon 81). Furthermore, the war effort helped to establish the superhero as an institution of North American popular culture. Gordon explains that, from 1941 to 1945, American servicemen purchased comic books more than any other reading material (Gordon 80). Comic books were precious to servicemen, being one of their most regular connections to home, and they reportedly "passed among the men until they fell apart" (Gordon 71). Furthermore, Gordon compares the status of comic books among servicemen to the idolization of pinup girls (Gordon 73). Since it has recently been demonstrated that soldiers held pinups as iconic representations of American womanhood and the soldiers' obligations to home,[10] he argues that the most popular comic book characters, like Superman and Batman, also served to remind soldiers of home and

---

[10] Gordon credits Robert Westbrook for establishing the iconic value of pinups for soldiers during the Second World War (Gordon 73).

"reinforce the purpose of the war in their minds" (Gordon 73-74). Gordon's argument here is congruous with Nietzsche's perspective on history. While Nietzsche asserts the importance of considering the values expressed in a culture's narratives, Gordon maintains that the values in a narrative actually influence its surrounding culture. To an extent, Gordon's argument even agrees with elements of Wertham's argument; not that reading comic books lead to delinquency, but that the values expressed in those narratives hold some influence over the values of their readership, for better or worse.

After considering Nietzsche's historiography, it is evident that the superhero's emergence into mainstream popular culture bears a tightly woven relationship to the Second World War. Contrary to Brooker's claims, both Superman and Batman held a significant role in the North American propaganda campaign during the Second World War. Since the most popular superheroes of the war effort adopted strong, responsible consumerist values, their following mythoi have built steadily upon those values and that style of crime fighting. However, although the modern superhero finds its cultural roots in consumerism, some recent storytellers have begun to challenge the superhero's traditional role of blindly supporting hegemonic values. An understanding of the origin of the modern superhero during the Second World War offers a deeper insight into narratives challenging the traditional superhero's values, such as Alan Moore's *Watchmen*, Frank Miller's *Dark Knight Returns*, Brad Meltzer's *Identity Crisis*, or Mark Millar's *Civil War*.

SILVER

Panels and Speech Balloons – From Wittgenstein to Wertham

The Graphic Language of Superhero Narratives

And

The Superhero Narrative's Influence on the Audience

The Graphic Language of Superhero Narratives

It is likely that when most people speak of language they think only of spoken and written language. Granted, speech and writing have many variations since there are innumerable foreign languages and dialects as well as various alphabets to transcribe these differently spoken languages. However, if what is intended by "language" is a means of communication, then, intuitively, speech and text do not exhaustively constitute the forms of language. There are many avenues of communication that are used fluently throughout everyday life which are left unconsidered in this base notion of language. An unknowing shrug of one's shoulders, an approving nod of one's head, the blowing whistle and waving hands of a traffic cop, the red octagon at an intersection, a green traffic light, raising a white flag during a battle, a fish wrapped in newspaper received from some nefarious Mafioso, or the diagrams of the emergency flight-safety pamphlet on airplanes – each of these serve communicative functions; yet, they are neglected in the common notion of language.

In addition to the common notion of language, philosophers have reflected upon the essence of language for centuries. While the basis of the general notion of language finds its roots in Plato and Aristotle, Ludwig Wittgenstein and Roland Barthes provide valuable insight in contemporary philosophy of language. Wittgenstein's account of language games in ordinary language use and Barthes' semiological approach to language, together, open up the traditional notion of language to include other forms of meaningful communication, such as including the language inherent to the sequential art of comics as recognized by Will Eisner and Scott McCloud. As such, through close examination it is apparent that Wittgenstein and Barthes successfully broaden the scope of language beyond speech and text to justify the inclusion of gesture, image, and sequential art. Here, I argue that, in light of Wittgenstein and Barthes, Eisner and McCloud's account of the language in comics is, appropriately, the recognition of an often neglected aspect in language's broad scope.

In analysing the role of gesture, image, and sequential art in language, the work of Will Eisner and Scott McCloud proves very insightful. Will Eisner is acknowledged as one of the greats in the comic book art. During the 40s, he had written and drawn the comic strip, *The Spirit*, which attained worldwide syndication, and later he pioneered the graphic novel art form with *A Contract with God*. In addition to these accomplishments, Eisner produced technical manuals for the U.S. Army and teaching material for schools. His most significant work in considering gesture, image, and sequential art as modes of language is *Comics and Sequential Art*. This work will help facilitate an understanding of gesture's role in language, in particular. Scott McCloud, on the other hand, is also regarded as an authority on comics. He has worked in comics since the mid 70s, but is mostly recognized for his critical works *Understanding Comics*, *Reinventing Comics*, and *Making Comics*. His book, *Understanding Comics*, is a thorough analysis of how comics function as a form of communication.

The distinction between language as speech and text and language as gesture, image, and sequential art is a misrepresentation of the inclusiveness of language. Early in Eisner's *Comics and Sequential Art* he acknowledges that the modern perspective of language regards words and images as independent disciplines, but that this separation is quite an arbitrary one (*Comics and Sequential Art* 13). A similar acknowledgement is found in McCloud's *Understanding Comics*. McCloud explains that sequential art

51

narratives are found throughout history, such as the pre-Columbian manuscript detailing the exploits of political and military hero 8-Deer "Tiger Claw" (McCloud 10), or the Bayeux Tapestry detailing the Norman's conquest of England (McCloud 12-13). These are effectively the forerunners to written text, as it is known today. Moreover, both Eisner and McCloud recognize that the line between this form of pictorial narrative and textual narrative becomes blurred when considering certain cases. For instance, early cave drawings use pictures to relate narratives (*Comics* 101). Furthermore, Egyptian hieroglyphics are drawings, but they do not resemble the subject; rather, they represent sounds, similar to modern alphabets (McCloud 12, Eisner *Comics* 101). In addition, Chinese letters are derived from pictographs, and thus they have some resemblance to their subject (*Comics* 14). With hieroglyphics and Chinese characters the distinction between text and image, or sequential art, is not so easily defined. Nevertheless, the Western notion of language generally concerns speech and text while dismissing gesture, image, and sequential art. Thus, this oversight must be addressed.

Since many contemporary notions of language find their roots in ancient philosophy, a brief consideration of ancient philosophy of language is helpful, in order to develop a foundation for this inquiry into the forms that constitute language. Plato's "Seventh Letter" and *Cratylus* make up most of this introduction to ancient philosophy of language, but Aristotle's *On Interpretation* is considered for its concise reflection on speech, text, and thought. In *On Interpretation*, Aristotle proposes that:

> Spoken words are the symbols of mental experience and written words are the symbols of spoken words. Just as all men have not the same writing, so all men have not the same speech sounds, but the mental experiences, which these directly symbolize, are the same for all, as also are those things of which our experiences are the images. (Aristotle 1.1)

Here, Aristotle recognizes that while spoken languages and alphabets differ, they all function to represent common thoughts and experiences. Aristotle also holds that images are recognizable to everyone since they are the reflection of common experiences. As such, Aristotle implies that the image can communicate to a far greater audience, since it is not bound by dialect or alphabet. Further, Martin Heidegger points out that Aristotle's classical passage illustrates the structure of language such that "the letters are signs of the sounds, the sounds are signs of the mental experiences, and these are signs of things" (Heidegger 97). For Aristotle, text does not resemble the appearance of the object it represents; rather, text reflects the sounds of speech. It is clear for Aristotle that writing is merely a means of representing what is said, thus speech takes priority over text. However, despite their varying degrees of separation, both speech and text attempt to represent and communicate thought. While a given experience equates to a universal thought for Aristotle, the expression of that thought in speech or text is subject to variation (such as foreign languages or different alphabets). However, while it is not the focus of his attention, Aristotle subtly affirms that the image is a greater communicator.

Plato maintains a similar notion on language as Aristotle's in the "Seventh Letter," but his view on language is expanded further in the *Cratylus*. Keep in mind that Plato is not known for explicitly expressing his ideas. Rather, his reputation is built upon the dialectic, elenchus, and aporia. However, in the "Seventh Letter" Plato puts forward a philosophical claim which he affirms as "true doctrine" ("Letters: VII" 342a). Since such a straightforward claim is so rare in Plato's texts, it bears a much heavier weight of significance than normal. Plato introduces a picture of our understanding in which he asserts that "first, we have a name, second, a description, third, an image, and fourth, a knowledge of the object" ("Letters: VII" 342b). In addition, Plato maintains "that we must put as a fifth the actual object of knowledge which is the true reality" ("Letters: VII" 342b). In Plato's account of knowledge here, the fifth is the object in the external world, the first three are mimetic representations of the fifth, and the fourth is our knowledge that aims towards the fifth. In this structure the first three – names, descriptions, and images – are a means of communicating the fourth – knowledge. Notice that Plato places the image closest to knowledge of the object in his hierarchy of knowledge. Perhaps these precise sentiments are the inspiration for Aristotle, who studied with Plato. This close relationship between the image and knowledge may indicate that Plato recognized images to hold a wider audience in communicating than either descriptions or names, since images speak beyond language barriers. Nevertheless, while Aristotle frequently differs from Plato on many issues, there are still elements of profound influence found in their philosophical works. As seen here, Plato and Aristotle share a peculiar favouritism towards the image in language.

In addition to this shared element between Plato and Aristotle, Plato further delves into the nature of language in the *Cratylus*. In this dialogue, Socrates, Hermogenes, and Cratylus interrogate whether there is a correctness of names or if names are social conventions. The first portion of the *Cratylus* is a discussion between Socrates and Hermogenes regarding the correctness of names. During this portion of the dialogue, Cratylus remains noticeably silent. Here, the discussion breaks down Greek words into syllables and letters in order to discern some common meaning to the sounds. In this discussion, Plato effectively anticipates linguistic theories regarding phonesthemes,[11]

---

[11] Phonesthemes are, theoretically, sounds in words that carry some small element of meaning that is common across other words; for instance *gl*- denotes a degree of light in *gl*eam, *gl*itter, *gl*ow, *gl*int, and *gl*isten.

which Socrates and Hermogenes suppose help to determine the meaning of names and words. The two investigate the meanings of names and words according to their form, their pronounciation, or their spelling. They wish to establish a correctness of names where the name itself carries information about that which it names.[12] However, once Cratylus enters the argument in the latter portion of the dialogue, Socrates begins to see the flaws in such an argument. In light of this, Socrates changes his position and asserts that there is a strong social element or convention in naming:

> I quite agree with you [Cratylus] that words should as far as possible resemble things, but I fear that this dragging in of resemblance, as Hermogenes says, is a shabby thing, which has to be supplemented by the mechanical aid of convention with a view to correctness. (*Cratylus* 435c)

Basically, Socrates claims that a representative language of likenesses would be ideal, but that this description does not reflect how people actually use language. In order to understand the use of language amongst people, Socrates requires that communal conventions must have an authoritative quality. This is reflected in that words, and their constituent syllables, do not actually resemble what they are used to represent; rather, the representative nature of words is the result of the social conventions of a community. Socrates goes on to say that "clearly he who first gave names gave them according to his conception of the things which they signified... and if his conception was erroneous, and he gave names according to his conception... [then we shall] be deceived by him" (*Cratylus* 436b). Here, Socrates' argument demonstrates that there is a level of arbitrariness in assigning names and also a social interdependence in learning names. The Socratic position acknowledges that there is an initial naming event and, from then onwards, a community of speakers learn names and their meanings from one another,

---

[12] However, it is important to note that the interlocutors do not analyze names and words according to how they appear. As such, they do not interrogate the appearance of the written form of a name to inquire whether it resembles the object to which it refers. The look of letters is of no concern in the *Cratylus*.

hence the erroneous beliefs would be passed on in Socrates' example. This aspect of Plato's account of language bears much in common with Saul A. Kripke's causal chain theory of reference presented in *Naming and Necessity*.[13] As with Aristotle, the concluding arguments of the *Cratylus* regard language as an expression of thought and as a communal function.

Together, the notion of language generated by Plato and Aristotle becomes the basis of the common notion of language. While both philosophers subtly acknowledged the communicative universality of the image, they focused on speech and text as the chief means of expressing thought. However, in both of these aspects, Plato and Aristotle expressed that language acts within a community. It is apparent that both of these philosophers interpreted language as a representational system used in a community. These ideas of language use in a community and the represented meanings in a language later become the focus of contemporary language philosophers such as Ludwig Wittgenstein and Roland Barthes. By interrogating Wittgenstein's notion of language games and Barthes' semiology of language, it is clear that "language" is a concept with forms beyond just speech and text.

While there is a communicative element to both Plato and Aristotle's accounts of language, it appears to be largely overlooked in the philosophy of language until Wittgenstein's *Philosophical Investigations* draws it to the forefront of academic attention. Wittgenstein's inquiries into ordinary language usage comes largely as a reaction to the analytical school, which viewed language merely as descriptive propositions and his *Tractatus Logico-Philosophicus* helped initiate this philosophical

---

[13] Kripke's causal chain theory of reference explicitly maintains that there is an initial baptism of the name, where the referent of the name is fixed either by ostension or description. Thereafter, the name and its referent are passed on to other speakers by means of continual deferral to other speakers, which eventually reaches back to the initial baptism (Kripke 96).

school. The *Philosophical Investigations* is Wittgenstein's attempt to rectify some of the "grave mistakes" of the *Tractatus* (Wittgenstein x). Wittgenstein utilizes the language game as the core concept of his *Philosophical Investigations*.

In the *Philosophical Investigations*, Wittgenstein considers ordinary language usage to illustrate how we use words and what meaning is intended in their use. For Wittgenstein, the language game is the socially understood context within which a word finds meaning (Wittgenstein S7, S47, S65). The social context of a language game need not be universal; rather, it could be a community of any size. For instance, how "red" can mean "a state of loss or indebtedness" in financial discourse, "radically left" or "communist" in political dialogue, or even "under fire" or "hostile" in military lingo. Each of these social dynamics constitutes a language game where the word can be easily understood to have a certain meaning within that particular context. If one were to ask a question that has no specified language game (or comes from one language game inquiring of another), then one cannot expect to understand or appreciate the answer (Wittgenstein S47). In this sense, one needs to be in tune with how a word is used in order to understand its meaning. In other words, one has to be a part of the active language game in order to successfully comprehend what is being communicated. According to Wittgenstein, the word's meaning is whatever the speaker intends and others, who are in on the language game, can best understand the word's meaning. Images are understood in these terms, as well. However, as Plato and Aristotle imply, images are generally accessible to a much broader audience than speech or text. Fittingly, the language game for an image that closely resembles its object is nearly universal. However, some images do not resemble their respective objects, such as with

57

abstract art. In a case where seemingly random geometric figures are grouped together and called a face, the image may only communicate such a message to a smaller community, one that has been schooled in such artistic styles.

For Wittgenstein, language games constitute our use of language. However, the language game is not arbitrary in the sense that it would be chaotic and useless; rather, the language game operates according to a dynamic set of rules. Language appeals to a set of rules which are neither eternal nor consistent. Instead, in using language, new rules are created and old rules are altered (Wittgenstein S83). This applies to both semantics and syntax. New meanings for words arise quite frequently as they are used in different contexts, such as "red" in financial, political, or military circles. The change in syntax is also observable. In academia, preference is currently given to short, concise sentences. In addition, the passive voice is disfavoured by some academic circles. The rules that semantics and syntax adhere to are derived from language use. Wittgenstein claims that understanding a sentence relies on adhering to rules (Wittgenstein S81). These rules are essentially social conventions. They arise and operate in a social environment. Keep in mind that the rules of a language game are not static; instead, they are dynamic and malleable. Both the meaning of words and structure of sentences are open to change, given that there is a community of speakers that accept and maintain the change. Likewise, Wittgenstein's account of rules in language also applies to the image. As with the earlier example, the malleability and evolution of these rules allows for the development of new styles of depicting images. Those who are familiar with the particular rules will best understand what is communicated through either speech, text, or image. Communication is successful because language adheres to these dynamic and malleable rules.

In the context of Wittgenstein's language game, we should consider whether the ordinary person and the philosopher use the word "language" in two separate language games. It was mentioned in the opening paragraph of this paper that there appears to be a difference between the ordinary person's notion of language and the philosopher's view. However, perhaps the ordinary person and the philosopher are not using two different senses of the term "language," as if they intend different two meanings. Suppose the ordinary person considers language and thinks of English, French, Chinese, Swahili, and so forth, while the philosopher considers language and thinks of speech acts, writing, analytical propositions, mathematics, propositional logic, and so on. At first glance, it would appear that the ordinary person and the philosopher employ two different senses of the term "language." However, I think that Wittgenstein would argue that they are not utilizing "language" in two different language games. Consider the likelihood that they are both using the same sense of the term, but that only the examples readily coming to mind differ. The ordinary person and the philosopher may very well intend the same meaning of "language," yet they think of different examples since they have spent varying amounts of reflection on the matter. The "language" of philosophers and ordinary people should not be regarded as separate meanings in differing language games. Furthermore, the communicative nature of the examples associated with language would imply that the meaning of language is tied heavily to communication.

Following from the social and communicative nature of Wittgenstein's language games, we shall turn next to consider Roland Barthes' semiotics. Wittgenstein emphatically instates the necessary social context of language, exposing that language is more than representational. However, Barthes brings the social and representational aspects of language together harmoniously in his semiotic approach to language. Barthes focuses his analyses on the meaning of signs and symbols. As such, we shall see that Barthes helps open up the scope of language beyond speech and text, to include gesture and imagery.

Barthes' semiotic approach to language is very non-restrictive. In *Mythologies*, he regards language as the following:

> We shall take *language, discourse, speech*, etc., to mean any significant unit or synthesis, whether verbal or visual: a photograph will be a kind of speech for us in the same way as a newspaper article; even objects will become speech, if they mean something. (Barthes 110-111)

In this sense, Barthes takes language to be anything which is a medium for communicating meaning. Here, language is considered as any means of conveying meaning from one person to another. Accordingly, speech, text, gesture, and image are equal across the plane of language. Furthermore, Barthes asserts that "any material can arbitrarily be endowed with meaning" (Barthes 110). As such, examples of language can be seen in a green traffic light, a raised, white flag during battle, or a fish wrapped in newspaper received from a notorious gangster. These objects deliver meaning in their given contexts. Moreover, these objects essentially take on the form of gestures. A green traffic light carries the same meaning as a traffic officer who signals to a driver to continue on. A raised, white flag signals surrender on the battlefield to the same extent as a communiqué in Morse code. The dead fish from a mobster signifies a death threat or, perhaps more specifically, a threat that the receiver will soon sleep with the fishes. In Barthes' semiotic terminology the green traffic light, white flag, and dead fish are empty signifiers until the social context attaches a meaning or concept to the signifier. The concept – continue driving, surrender, or death threat – is called the signified. Together, when the token signifier is combined with the socially determined signified, the synthesis is a sign (Barthes 112-113). The signifier, signified, and sign make up the elements of language in a semiological approach. Words, both written and spoken, operate within this system as well. Words are merely empty signifiers until a social significance is bestowed upon them. Only then do words become signs. This is best understood when considering neologisms such as "Viagra" or "hyperlink." These words, written or spoken, are empty to anyone who is not familiar with their use. Both pharmaceuticals and cyberspace utilize many new names and words, and unless one is familiar with their context and usage, then one is lost as to their significance.

In Barthes' semiotic approach to language, parallels with Wittgenstein's language game are blatantly apparent. Barthes claims that meaning in language arises from a history of use and not from "the nature of things" (Barthes 110) is unmistakably similar to Wittgenstein's language game. The importance of the social communicability of meaning runs through both of their philosophies of language. However, Barthes provides a much broader interpretation of the scope of language than Wittgenstein does, thus it finds greater applicability here. Both Barthes and Wittgenstein seem to agree that language operates within a social context, and that successful communication of meaning relies on this social context. Nevertheless, Barthes adopts an empirical approach to language with a broad scope, whereas Wittgenstein deals with "ordinary language usage" primarily as language is manifest in speech and text. Through using these philosophical perspectives in conjunction, it becomes much easier to analyse how gesture, image, and sequential art function as and contribute to language.

In order to dissect the role of image and sequential art in language, first we must interrogate gestures and postures, commonly known as "body language." Since much of the visually communicated library deals with human emotion, interaction, and narrative, an understanding of the communicative aspect of people's gestures is integral to an analysis of image and sequential art. Will Eisner maintains that people's emotionally invested gestures and expressive postures form a "non-verbal vocabulary of gesture" (*Comics* 100). While multiple gestures can communicate the same basic meaning,[14] they are also highly sensitive to context.[15] Furthermore, there is a mutually influential relationship between the gesture and the context. In a given situation, the gesture modifies the meaning of the utterance. For instance, the first panel's gesture in Figure 4 communicates an unsure apology; the third panel, a smug admission and apology; the fifth, a stubborn, insincere apology; the seventh, a shameful apology; the eighth, an apology of overwhelming frustration. Here, the gesture takes primacy over the text in communicating meaning (*Comics* 103). In this sense, the gesture almost acts as an adjective or an adverb that modifies the statement. However, the situation, or social context, of a given situation also modifies the meaning of the gesture. Taking Figure 5 as an example, the basic gesture remains constant throughout the panels, yet the meaning

---

[14] Please see Figure 3 for an example.
[15] Please see Figures 4 and 5 for examples.

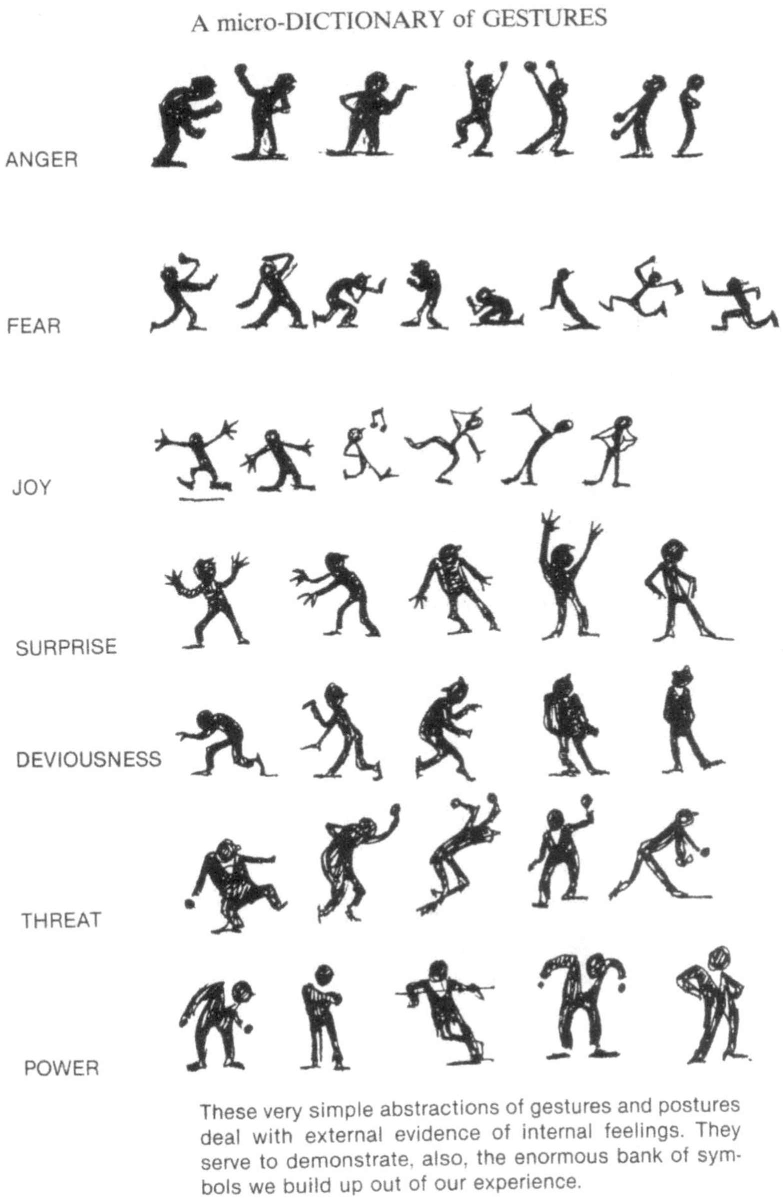
A micro-DICTIONARY of GESTURES
ANGER
FEAR
JOY
SURPRISE
DEVIOUSNESS
THREAT
POWER
These very simple abstractions of gestures and postures deal with external evidence of internal feelings. They serve to demonstrate, also, the enormous bank of symbols we build up out of our experience.

Figure 3: A micro-dictionary of gestures (Comics 102).

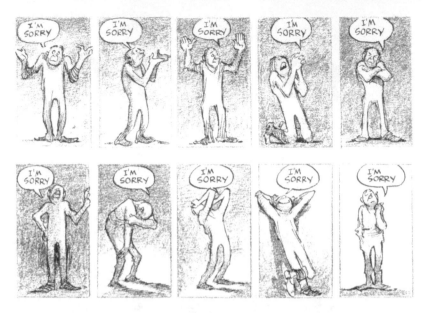

Figure 4: Speech modified by posture (Comics 103).

This basic symbol, derived from a familiar attitude, is amplified by words, costume, background and interaction (with another symbolic posture) to communicate meanings and emotion.

Figure 5: Posture modified by surrounding context (Comics 16).

differs based on the subject's environment, the social context of the situation. For instance, the second panel's gesture in Figure 5 communicates a subject who is indifferent to the woman's lecturing; the third panel depicts a subject who is asleep and unaware of any threat; the fourth, a disbelieving judge; and the fifth, a worried sick subject waiting with the patient. In each of the cases in Figure 5, the social context modifies the meaning communicated by the gesture. This account of gesture lends itself aptly to both Barthes' and Wittgenstein's accounts of language. Eisner's account of gesture is entirely cohesive with Barthes'. Recall that Barthes affirms that language is made up of signifiers, signifieds, and signs (Barthes 112-113). Accordingly, Eisner's account of gesture can be interpreted such that the person's posture is the empty signifier, the meaning is the signified, and together they make up the sign, or the gesture. However, the meaning of a gesture is influenced by the social context, as well. Here, Wittgenstein's language game helps shed light on the matter of gesture as language. Wittgenstein asserts that the language game is the social context that determines the use and meaning of words (Wittgenstein S7, S47, S65). It is evident that the language game operates beyond the scope of words as they are spoken or written, and that meaning communicated through gesture functions in this same manner. Gesture is affected by social context just like words are affected in the language game. In synthesis, Eisner, Barthes, and Wittgenstein help affirm that gesture is a significant mode of language.

Following the role of gesture in language, we may presently interrogate the roles of image and sequential art. It should come as no surprise that image is a mode of language. In the *Cratylus*, Plato frequently compares language to painting. Near the conclusion of the dialectic, Socrates reminds Cratylus, "Have we not several times acknowledged that names rightly given are the likenesses and images of the things which they name" (*Cratylus* 439a). Since Plato's account of language is mimetic, the comparison to the painting or image is straightforward. For Plato, speech and text aims to be representative, but it relies on social conventions (*Cratylus* 435c). Now, when considering the image as a part of language, the representative aspect increases since the images typically bear a resemblance to the objects they represent. Plato acknowledges in the *Cratylus* that if an image expresses every point of the reality of the object, then it would no longer be an image, but an exact duplicate, copy, or clone (*Cratylus* 432b). Indeed, an image is not an exact duplicate of the object, it is something that resembles and represents a given object. Scott McCloud reflects the representative quality of images quite concisely. In *Understanding Comics*, McCloud discusses Magritte's painting "The Treachery of Images."[16] The painting is of a pipe and there is an inscription in French that roughly translates to "This is not a pipe." Certainly, the image is not a pipe; the original painting is a painted representation of a pipe, while the image in McCloud's book is a mass-produced, printed copy of multiple, hand-drawn reproductions of a painted representation of a pipe (McCloud 24-25). Images are highly representative, but images vary in the degree to which they resemble their representative objects. McCloud uses a scale of various degrees of resemblance. For instance, photographs of people provide a high degree of resemblance, while simple stick drawings are such a vague resemblance that they could be said to resemble nearly anyone (McCloud 31).[17] These images vary in terms of realistic resemblance to abstract resemblance. However, following the abstract stick drawings, McCloud surmises that words, descriptions,

---

[16] Please see Figure 6.
[17] Please see Figure 7.

Figure 6: This is not a pipe (McCloud 24).

Figure 7: From realistic to more abstracted (McCloud 31).

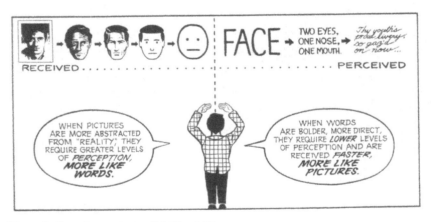

Figure 8: From images to text (McCloud 49).

68

and metaphors continue the spectrum into the abstract realm (McCloud 49).[18] In this sense, the separation between images and words breaks down, and these two modes of language, traditionally held apart, come closer together. Images and words both communicate meanings, but perhaps the most significant difference is that images function with a higher degree of resemblance and lower degree of social convention than words. McCloud argues that since images are received information, the message is instantaneous, and since words are perceived information, we need to be literate in order to interpret the words (McCloud 49). However, while this may not be an entirely accurate description how we process images and words, especially from a Barthesian perspective, McCloud does seem to strike on an intuitive distinction between images and words. His claim here is gravely mistaken. Whether we see the images, read the text, or hear the speech, both the image and the word are subject to sensation and perception. Essentially, both image and word must be received and perceived. Furthermore, from a Barthesian perspective, images are more universal, or they participate in a much larger social context, than words. When images resemble their objects, their meaning can be communicated to a much larger audience since most people will recognize the resemblance. This is not the case with words largely due to language barriers and illiteracy. This distinction is evident in Figure 8, where it should be safe to say that the images could easily cross cultural boundaries and language barriers, while the text is quickly prohibited by such barriers. This is, precisely, Aristotle's implication in *On Interpretation* (Aristotle 1.1). It is not surprising to see Wittgenstein's language game in effect here, as well. Both images and words are subject to their social contexts. In this case, the images of a person's face take part in a nearly universal language game, while

---

[18] Please see Figure 8.

69

the written word "face" can only participate in the language game of literate English speakers. As in the case of gesture, it is evident that Wittgenstein's language game applies to aspects of language beyond merely speech and text. Nevertheless, given the Barthesian perspective and considering Wittgenstein's language game, McCloud's intuition that images and words exist on a scale still carries intuitive validity. Both images and words communicate meaning, just through different means. Although McCloud fails to recognize here that images and words are both received through sensation and both subject to perception, it seems that the scale he is trying to express really relies on the universal communicability of the meaning in the image or the word. This latter view is not so problematic.

The solitary image can communicate a message, but sequential art can communicate a narrative. Eisner defines sequential art simply as "a train of images deployed in sequence" (Eisner *Graphic Storytelling* 6). However, McCloud's account of sequential art is preferable to Eisner's since McCloud refers to images juxtaposed spatially, such as those found in comic strips, and not images juxtaposed temporally, such as those of film and television (McCloud 7). This distinction is important here, since this paper does not truly delve into how animation and film operate as language. While sequential art and the motion picture share much in common, there are likely significant nuances to each form which may be lost in translation. However, film has had a very short history in comparison to sequential art. Since sequential art can be traced back through the ages for thousands of years, it garners attention here in lieu of film. Thus, the sequential art common to the comic strip, comic book, and graphic novel is the focus of investigation.

The narrative capability of sequential art goes well beyond that of the solitary image. While a solitary image can communicate meaning, by adding a related image in sequence more information is communicated than that contained by the two images – meaning is found in the gutter, as well. The gutter is the term for the space between panels in a comic; it is the gap between the images. Between the images in sequential art, time, motion, and action are implied. Moreover, the gutters in sequential art force the reader to participate in the action.[19] In Figure 9, there are two panels which imply an axe murder; but, exactly how the murder occurs or how the scream sounds is left up to the imagination of the reader (McCloud 68). McCloud calls this effect "closure;" it is the "phenomenon of observing the parts but perceiving the whole" (McCloud 63).[20] While there are varying types of closure, essentially, the reader interpolates the implied action from seeing the images provided by the author/artist. In a sense, this gives new meaning to the saying "read between the lines." Eisner argues that the gutter seeks to communicate a sense of time passing and the actions that occupy those moments that are unseen between the panels (*Comics* 107).[21] Since the reader must participate in the narrative of sequential art, this can be interpreted as a means of participating in the language game of the images and gutters. The use of panels and gutters has not always been the standard in narrative, sequential art. The picture manuscript that depicted 8-deer "Tiger's-Claw," the Bayeux Tapestry, and ancient cave drawings did not utilize the panel-gutter convention. This convention has developed as printed comics became more commonplace, and the convention is still being manipulated and experimented upon.[22]

---

[19] Please see Figure 9.
[20] Please see Figure 10.
[21] Please see Figure 11.
[22] Please see Figures 12 and 13.

Figure 9: The gutter (McCloud 68).

Figure 10: Closure (McCloud 64).

Figure 11: Intermediate action (Comics 107).

Figure 12: Sequence in a divided panel (Perkins *Captain America #23* 3).

Figure 13: Sequence in a single panel (Perkins Captain America #24 14).

Figures 12 and 13 both portray a characters movement; however, Figure 12 utilizes panels and gutters, while the movement in Figure 13 is expressed in one contained panel. The use of multiple panels in Figure 12 intuitively implies that, although the figure in the background quickly sneaks over to the security door, he stops to hide along the way. In the second panel, the character has hidden again, and the third panel shows him dash away. The quickness of his stealthy dash is emphasized by the lack of movement from the character in the foreground. Figure 12 implies very quick, staccato movements overall. Figure 13 depicts similarly quick movements. The character, which begins in the background, has just leaped out of a window to an adjacent rooftop. The character is shown in three positions: flipping through the air; preparing to land on the roof; and, following through across the roof. Since this movement is contained in a single panel, it implies a more fluid and graceful motion. While the panel-gutter convention may or may not be utilized, it is still a convention that can be manipulated to modify what is communicated in the narrative. Wittgenstein's comments on the dynamic use and evolution of rules (Wittgenstein S83) reflect how the panel-gutter convention can be manipulated to produce such effects. In addition, the conventional panels and gutters in comics provide an easy to follow system for reading sequential art.

To some degree, it is almost as if the images provide the semantics of sequential art, while the panels provide the syntax. Images communicate meaning through representation and gesture. Panels and gutters provide a system of combining the images like words in a sentence, or sentences in a paragraph. Furthermore, through the combination of words and images in sequential art, the narrative attains a higher degree of successful communication. The image communicates an enormous amount of information through its likeness and gesture, while the text can focus on dialogue or the thoughts of characters. Since the image can communicate the description of the scene, the characters, the action, and the emotional sentiment, the dialogue can focus on communicating discourse and reflection.

Language is misrepresented when only speech and text are considered. Gesture, image, and sequential art represent a truly significant portion of language. While the image warrants a subtle nod of respect in both Plato and Aristotle, its importance has been since overlooked. Plato holds the image next to knowledge ("Letters: VII" 342b), and Aristotle maintains that it communicates nearly universally (Aristotle 1.1). Nevertheless, philosophers and common folk have been preoccupied with language as primarily speech and text. In contemporary philosophy of language, however, the door is cracked ajar for gesture, image, and sequential art to re-enter the public notion of the scope of language. While Wittgenstein emphasizes ordinary language use with the language game (Wittgenstein S7, S47, S65) and dynamic rule-following (Wittgenstein S83), Barthes helps us to acknowledge that meaning is communicated by innumerable means (Barthes 110). Together, Wittgenstein and Barthes bring attention back to the socially communicative function of language, thus expanding the conception of language's scope to accept gesture, image, and sequential art. Furthermore, by applying the philosophies of Wittgenstein and Barthes to the analyses of Eisner and McCloud, it is evident that gesture, image, and sequential art function as language. Thus, the common notion of language is insufficient. Each of speech, text, gesture, image, and sequential art is justified under the inclusiveness of language.

Art's Influence on its Audience

After the high school massacre at Columbine in Littleton, Colorado, investigators seized the killers' computers and music collections in order to determine their influence. Such investigations commonly attempt to link artists like Marilyn Manson or videogames such as *Grand Theft Auto* to acts of terrible violence. While many people criticize the approach which simply blames the media, perhaps there is some modicum of method in this madness. The notion that we are products of our environment is not far-fetched. Nevertheless, most people claim either that mass media has no influence over the individual or, alternatively, that mass media can be the direct cause of an individual's corruption. Both are extreme viewpoints which oversimplify a complex matter. Through an analysis of the crusade against comics, it is apparent that art is communicative and that censorship is an attempt to regulate art's messages according to some moral status quo (however misguided that may be). The crusade against comics from the 1940s to the mid-50s serves here as a representative case study for the arguments surrounding the censorship of mass media.

In order to proceed in this analysis on aesthetics, the boundaries of art must be clarified. While the qualifications for art may be highly debatable, an analysis of this nature requires that one take a stance on the issue. As such, the stance represented here is a very broad interpretation of what qualifies as art. The aesthetic analysis which herein follows shall consider art in a similar manner as the Birmingham school of thought. As Dick Hebdidge notes in *Subculture, the Meaning of Style*, such aesthetic scholars endorsed the possibility that worthwhile aesthetic products may arise from the various forms of mass media (Hebdidge 8). In particular, this analysis adopts the aesthetic

77

qualifications for art that Scott McCloud describes in *Understanding Comics*. McCloud

asserts that art is any human activity which does not arise from either the human instinct

to survive or reproduce (McCloud 164). This perspective is quite broad indeed and

McCloud is not oblivious to this. He admits that this definition opens art's doors to

include art as self-expression, athletic endeavours, the foundations of language, science,

and philosophy, as well as the pursuit of truth and discovery (McCloud 167). As such,

McCloud's aesthetic qualification of art enthusiastically encompasses the possibilities of

mass media.

Before considering how censorship functions as art's manifestation of morals, it is

important to develop the foundation on which art is seen as necessarily communicative.

Here, analysis will focus on Roland Barthes' *Mythologies* and Umberto Eco's *A Theory*

of Semiotics. Considering these texts, their prominent arguments suggest that art is

necessarily communicative. Incidentally, that art is communicative is a consequence of

accepting the premises of semiotics in general. For Barthes, the signifier is the intended

idea, the sign is the idea made manifest in language, and the signified is the idea received

(Barthes 113). In Barthes' approach to semiotics, one meets the open approach that

semiotics applies to all forms of communication, beyond just spoken and written

language, and including art. Barthes proposes the following:

> We shall therefore take *language, discourse, speech*, etc., to mean any significant unit or
> synthesis, whether verbal or visual: a photograph will be a kind of speech for us in the
> same way as a newspaper article; even objects will become speech, if they mean
> something. (Barthes 110-111)

Here, since visual culture is implicated in Barthes' argument, we see that semiotics has

the potential to be applied to art as a form of communication. Other semioticians share

this position, as well. In *A Theory of Semiotics*, Umberto Eco maintains that "semiotics studies all cultural processes as *processes of communication*" (Eco 8). Eco further

supports Barthes' claim in the following comments:

> In culture every entity can become a semiotic phenomenon. The laws of signification are the laws of culture. For this reason culture allows a continuous process of communicative exchanges... *Culture can be studied completely under a semiotic profile.* (Eco 28)

In this sense, any meaningful artistic expression can be seen as a means of

communication. Additionally, the semiotic triad of signifier, sign, and signified

accommodates the intention of the artist, the independent art object, and the interpretation

of the audience. However, the semiotic approach is not merely potentially applicable to

art; rather, it appears that art is always a subject for semiotic analysis and, thus, it is

necessarily a communicative medium. The audience experience of a work of art renders

it a communicative act, regardless of artist intention or any element of the independent art

object. Furthermore, Eco's definition of a sign implies this same sense of importance

assigned to the audience. Eco defines a sign as "everything that, on the grounds of a

previously established social convention, *can be taken as* something standing for

something else" (Eco 16, emphasis added). Eco's definition of a sign relies on an

audience as a prerequisite for a signifier to be taken as anything. This is also the case

when considering artistic works. Because the audience is involved with the artwork –

even in the most minor way – in this relation of signifier to signified, the artwork is

necessarily an act of communication.

Having developed a foundation for viewing art as communication, this analysis

can now turn to the crusade against comics. While considering the crusade against

comics as a case of censorship over mass media, keep in mind that the art we consume

through mass media is communicative and, as such, there must be a message that is communicated through the work of art. Amy Kiste Nyberg's *Seal of Approval: The History of the Comics Code* and Bart Beaty's *Fredric Wertham and the Critique of Mass Culture* provide much of the basis of this analysis. Frederic Wertham's own works *Seduction of the Innocent* and "What are Comic Books?" are also analyzed here. In addition, Lynda Nead's *The Female Nude: Art, Obscenity and Sexuality* also provides some context for the debate on censoring mass media.

The crusade against comics provides a prototypical case of the arguments invoked in the debate over censoring mass media. The comic book was a new phenomenon in the 40s and 50s, and it faced the same problems that had been faced with the introduction of the dime novel, the comic strip, and film (Nyberg 1). Since anti-vice representation campaigns had already driven much of the pornographic material underground, they had broadened their scope to obscenity in various media (Nyberg 2). Accordingly, comics came under the scrutiny of those concerned with representations of vice in media. The newfound success of Superman amongst children led to publishers flooding the market with superhero comics (Nyberg 5). However, shortly after World War II, the public had largely lost interest in superhero comics, and the dominant genre of comic books shifted towards the crime and horror stories of pulp fiction (Nyberg 17). The shift from superheroes to crime and horror brought previously mild criticism to a furious zenith (Nyberg 17). These crime comics were to become the target of seemingly inexhaustible criticism and attack. The crusade against comics, which followed in the post-war era, is dominated by the criticism of Dr. Fredric Wertham, psychiatrist and expert on juvenile delinquency, and by the introduction of the comics code, the comic publishers' means of self-censorship.

Undoubtedly, the most recognizable figure of the comics crusade was Dr. Frederic Wertham. At best, Wertham was generally considered a pariah amongst academics and, at worst, a doom-bringer for fans of comics. Wertham wrote extensively on the so-called evils of comic books including numerous journal and magazine articles. However, his arguments against comics climaxed in his book *Seduction of the Innocent*. Wertham advocated an interdisciplinary approach to analyzing media effects involving psychiatry, psychology, sociology, economics, biology, and history (Nyberg 101). According to Beaty, Wertham defined his own approach as "an analysis of typical cases: an analysis of comic books, an analysis of the scientific problems involved, an analysis of the methods of the comic book publishers, and an analysis of the practical steps that could be taken to address the findings of these analyses" (Beaty 132). Wertham admits that *Seduction of the Innocent* was never intended to be a scholarly text; instead he wished to address a lay readership (Beaty 133, Nyberg 93). However, this allowed Wertham to preach against comics while going unchecked by his academic peers. According to Nyberg, "The book was not an objective overview of the comic book industry but a deliberately sensationalized portrait of the worst that comic books had to offer" (Nyberg 93). Furthermore, unlike many critics of comics who focused on crime and horror comics, Wertham employed the term "crime comics" to include "comic books that depict crime, whether the setting is urban, Western, science-fiction, jungle, adventure or the realm of supermen" (Wertham 20). Most critics considered crime comics to be those comics that depicted crime realistically and in detail, comics such as *True Crime* or *Crime SuspenStories*. For Wertham, however, the term encompassed many other comic book genres and titles. Additionally, Wertham focused on particular isolated comics within the

81

crime and horror genres, but spoke broadly about all comics in general. Armed with extreme examples, regardless of whether they were exceptional or not, Wertham attacked the entire comics medium.

Nevertheless, Wertham's attack on comics proceeded according to a certain methodology. As a psychiatrist, Wertham employed what he termed the "clinical method,' which consisted of "detailed case histories, observation, and follow-up" (Nyberg x). The only effective way to study long-term media effects, Wertham argued, was according to his clinical method (Nyberg x). While this approach must seem natural for a psychiatrist, many media scholars dismissed his work as unsophisticated social science that lacked quantifiable, supporting evidence (Nyberg x). Despite a lack of support from his academic peers, Wertham persistently presented arguments that comics provided a significant influence on children that led to delinquent behaviour. Wertham's typical argumentation is exemplified in this passage:

> Some fathers have told me that it "hasn't done any harm to my child; after all, when he reads *Hamlet* [italics added] he doesn't see ghosts and want to put poison in my ear." The answer is easy: first of all, comic books are not as artistic as *Hamlet* [italics added]. Second, there's only one *Hamlet* [italics added] (and most children don't read it), whereas comic books come by the millions. Third, there has been no other literature for adults or for children in the history of the world, at any period or in any nation, that showed in pictures and in words, over and over again, half-nude girls, in all positions being branded, burned, bound, tied to wheels, blinded, pressed between spikes, thrown to snakes and wild animals, crushed with rocks, slowly drowned or smothered, or having their veins punctured and their blood drawn off. (Wertham 396).

This passage ought to clearly convey the extent of Wertham's bias against comics. Although this passage is full of specious arguments against comics, his point about grotesque brutality may be the case in a handful of crime and horror comics; however, it is not the case in the vast majority of comic books, and to lead someone to believe that it is so is entirely misleading and a gross abuse of his own authority as a psychiatrist.

However, even with all of his prejudices and fallacious arguments, a valid point remains central to Wertham's arguments against the negative influences of mass media. Wertham's typical bias is still transparent in *Seduction of the Innocent* when he lists the potentially negative mass conditioning that comics exert upon their audience:

1) The comic book format is an invitation to illiteracy.
2) Crime comic books create an atmosphere of cruelty and deceit.
3) They create a readiness for temptation.
4) They stimulate unwholesome fantasies.
5) They suggest criminal or sexually abnormal ideas.
6) They furnish the rationalization for [those criminal or sexually abnormal ideas], which may be ethically even more harmful than the impulse.
7) They suggest the forms of a delinquent impulse may take and supply details of technique.
8) They may tip the scales toward maladjustment or delinquency. (Wertham 118)

Essentially, Wertham blames the entire medium of comics for some of its content. Nevertheless, while Wertham's aesthetic bias taints his analysis, it remains relevant that points 6, 7, and 8 actually account for the stories depicted in some crime and horror comics. Once one sifts through the critic's own prejudices towards comics as a medium, there remains a valid point that if crime and horror comics portray such events, then this message may influence an individual who is reading the work. Despite Wertham's broad claims and cultural elitism, the heart of his argument is actually persuasive, insisting that the messages of mass media can potentially influence the audience.

Although comic books were a favoured scapegoat for Wertham, his criticism was not limited to this medium only. For instance, Wertham advocated self-censorship for newspaper publishers and journalists to use restraint in publicizing sensational crimes, and, according to Nyberg, arguing that "immature readers, especially children, needed to be protected from society" (Nyberg 88). Furthermore, Wertham criticized media coverage of the Vietnam War, as well, arguing that the government employed it as a

83

commercial for the army (Nyberg 102). According to Nyberg's account, Wertham also

felt that the government and the Surgeon General were suppressing research

demonstrating the adverse effects of violence, brutality, and sadism portrayed in the

media (Nyberg 102). He also maintained that the government blamed the individual or

the audience, and not the producers of products that sensationalized violence (Nyberg

102). It is important to realize and remember that while Wertham focused his attention

on chastising the cultural value of comics, he did not exclude other means of negative

influence in mass media. He clearly reminds his audience of this in chapter six of

Seduction of the Innocent:

> Even more than crime, juvenile delinquency reflects the social values of current in a
> society. Both adults and children absorb these social values in their daily lives, at home,
> in school, at work, and also in all the communications imparted as entertainment,
> instruction or propaganda through mass media, from the printed word to television.
> (Wertham 149)

The soundest portion of Wertham's heated criticism is that art is a mode of

communication. As we take in art as entertainment, we take in its messages constantly

and the content of art's messages may influence us. Additionally, Nyberg explains

Wertham's position as follows:

> Children who were exposed to a steady diet of comic books and other violent material
> learned that such behaviour was socially acceptable and put these lessons into practice.
> Wertham shifted the blame from the individual to the environment: comic books didn't
> make children delinquent, but [they] were part of a cultural matrix that normalized
> delinquent behaviour in the minds of children. (Nyberg 97)

Nyberg further explains that:

> Wertham's generalized critique of mass culture focused on the way that mass culture
> mediated between the child and his environment. [Wertham] identified the problem as a
> social one that extended far beyond the publication of comic books. (Nyberg 97)

84

Wertham's arguments are clearly not restricted to the influence of comic books; rather, he regards the whole of mass culture susceptible to impressing negative attitudes upon the individual.

Furthermore, many other academics and intellectuals share Wertham's position. Sentiments similar to Wertham's are even found in Ancient Greek philosophy. In the *Republic*, Plato also emphasizes that, in youth especially, mythic tales make an impression on a person's character (Plato 2.377b), and he further claims that, in education, "we must begin... by a censorship over our story-makers, and what they do well we must pass and what not, reject" (Plato 2.377c). It is clear that Plato holds that myths influence moral character. This is further evident in the effort the interlocutors spend in encouraging rigorous censorship of mythic tales of gods and heroes. Plato's sentiments on the influence of art's message on its audience are evidence of the timelessness of this intuition.[23] Furthermore, more contemporary authorities reflect Wertham's sentiments, as well. Beaty recounts the position of the Federal Bureau of Investigation's director, J. Edgar Hoover, on the topic, which affirms that comics portraying a true anticrime sentiment are actually educational, but adding the reservation that:

> Crime books, comics and other stories packed with criminal activity and presented in such a way as to glorify crime and the criminal may be dangerous, particularly in the hands of an unstable child. A comic book which is replete with the lurid and macabre; which places the criminal in a unique position by making him a hero; which makes lawlessness attractive; which ridicules decency and honesty; which leaves the impression that graft and corruption are necessary evils of American life; which depicts the life of the criminal as exciting and glamorous may influence the susceptible boy or girl who already possesses anti-social tendencies. (Beaty 127)

---

[23] Also, note the irony of Plato's sentiments that art's message may influence its audience and the circumstances surrounding the death of Socrates. Those who condemned Socrates for corrupting the youth also share some notion of the message's persuasive influence over the audience.

Hoover's sentiments reflect Wertham's own in the sense that the message of the work has the potential to be influential on its audience. However, Hoover acknowledges that the content of the message may be either positive or negative, and if the message is of a positive nature, then the resulting influence is beneficial to the overall well-being of the individual and the community at large. Additionally, Nead reports President Nixon's sentiments on a similar matter. When the Commission on Obscenity and Pornography rejected any correlation between viewing pornography and committing acts of sexual violence, Nixon responded as follows on 25 October 1970:

> The Commission contends that the proliferation of filthy books and plays has no lasting harmful effect on a man's character. If that be true, it must also be true that great books, great paintings and great plays have no ennobling effect on a man's conduct. Centuries of civilization and ten minutes of common sense tell us otherwise. (Nead 488)

Nixon's response to the Commission contextualizes the matter plainly and straightforwardly – if no ill influence can be communicated to the audience through art, then neither can any good influence be communicated, and that simply contradicts centuries of valuing art. As Nixon appeals to common sense, the truth of his comments strikes us as obvious, intuitive, and undeniable. Ultimately, Nixon's sentiments also correspond to Wertham's own position which lies underneath his passionate argumentation. This position is evidently both intuitive and timeless. As such, at the very least, there is some credibility to Wertham's arguments in so far as they concern only that entertainment in mass media carries a potentially influential message.

As a medium for artistic communication, comics deliver a message that has the potential to influence its audience. Accordingly, any censorship of the comics medium is an attempt to restrict certain messages from being expressed. Since the comics code never adopted an age-based system of regulations, the form of censorship adopted by the comics publishers was content oriented. As such, whereas censorship is a means of controlling the content of the medium, the guiding force of this censorship must be some set of value judgements and morals. However, in this case, and as is too often the case, the authority in control of censorship employs a strictly conservative set of morals. This results in a very restrictive form of censorship, which usually maintains the status quo alongside a political or religious agenda. This is what happened in the case of comics during the comics crusade, although it did not fully satisfy Wertham's demands for action against depictions of violence in mass media entertainment. Nevertheless, it must be clear that censorship is an attempt to regulate art's messages according to some moral set, even if that moral set is not democratically representative of the populace's beliefs. Censorship is employed as a means to ensure moral qualities in the public. Such a position is supported by scholarly work through the ages, including Plato's *Republic* and Bronislaw Malinowski's work in anthropology. Moreover, that art's message is potentially influential is also the fundamental premise behind advertising and propaganda.

The influence of mass media on the individual is undeniable. Through an analysis of the crusade against comics, it is apparent that art is necessarily communicative and that censorship is an attempt to regulate the artistic message according to a moral set, however imperfect. While mass media is not the only environmental influence on a person's character, it is nevertheless an influence to some degree. People have blamed the media for corrupting the youth, and it appears that there is some modicum of method in this madness. As commercial advertising and political propaganda are bombarding us, we ought to be conscious of the media's potential influence on our attitudes, beliefs, and actions. Furthermore, we ought to be aware of the influence that messages in entertainment have on others as well as ourselves. Since mass media has encroached upon nearly every aspect of our lives in North America, we may very well have become products of our environment.

BRONZE

Heroes or Watchmen? – Contemporary Superhero Discourse

Justice and the Exceptional Character of the Superhero,

Defending the Imperfect Utopia,

And

Post-9/11 Discourse in *Civil War*

Justice and the Exceptional Character of the Superhero

Superheroes not only fascinate us with their fantastic powers, feats of strength, or heroic adventures, but they capture our imagination simply through their unyielding propensity to do good. Of course, not every superhero is a paragon of virtue, but it is nevertheless their virtuous qualities which intrigue us the most. When confronted by impending doom or a sadistic choice, how does the superhero summon the strength and commitment to justice to do the right thing? Perhaps the most perplexing question we ask ourselves about superheroes is, as Jeff Brenzel puts it, "why would people with these kinds of powers be so good?" (Brenzel 148). Philosophers have asked this question, as well, since at least as long ago as Plato's time. However, the question persists today, especially when we are confronted by news stories in the media of people using their great power for selfish and greedy ends, whether it is a corporation's exploitation of a desperate workforce or a country's military exploitation of another country's resources. So, why does power corrupt, and how do superheroes remain immune to the corruption of their power? This may not be immediately and indisputably answerable. Nonetheless, in order to facilitate an understanding of the superhero's exceptionally just character, I examine the treatment of selfishness in Plato's *Republic*, demonstrate the selfishness allowed by the limited liability of the modern corporation, and reflect upon the superhero characters Iron Man and Batman, particularly their depiction in recent film. As such, this essay examines how the superhero often acts contrary to typical selfish desires which might come with incredible power; instead they uphold an uncompromising responsibility and duty to society.

In order to better appreciate the view that people tend to act selfishly, we ought to first consider Plato's account of selfishness in the *Republic*. Plato's *Republic* is largely the search for an account of justice. Book I contains relatively weak arguments by both Socrates and Thrasymachus about whether or not it pays better to live a life of injustice rather than a just one. Summarily, Socrates argues that the function of the soul is to live well and, to live well, the soul must maintain its virtue, justice (Plato 1.353d – 353e). Book II begins as Glaucon is unsatisfied with the resolution of the previous debate, thus he acts as devil's advocate and pressures Socrates to further defend the status quo of justice (Plato 2.358c).

Glaucon begins by picking up where Thrasymachus had left off; he proceeds to make a case for injustice's worth. Initially, he states an observation that "what people say is that to do wrong is, in itself, a desirable thing; on the other hand, it is not desirable at all to suffer wrong…" (Plato 2.358e). Further, Glaucon adds, "… justice is accepted as a compromise, and valued, not as good in itself, but for lack of power to do wrong…" (Plato 2.359b). These observations are quite persuasive as they appeal to common sense. No person would desire that which would bring harm or pain. Likewise, all people would seek out a means to reduce harm and pain that they might suffer. However, note that these simple precepts are based on a person's selfish nature.

The essentially selfish nature of man becomes more evident as Glaucon relates his analogy with the tale of the Ring of Gyges. The tale speaks of a shepherd, Gyges, who finds a magical talisman that can render him invisible (Plato 2.359e). Once Gyges has determined the function of the ring, he uses it for his own personal gain, seducing the Queen, and then seizing the throne (Plato 2.360a). Glaucon claims that if such magical devices were given to both a just person and an unjust person that they would both act in the same unjust manner (Plato 2.360c). He also claims, "No one, it is commonly believed, would have such iron strength of mind as to stand fast in doing right..." (Plato 2.360b). This analogy culminates with the claim that "Every man believes that wrongdoing pays him personally much better..." (Plato 2.360d).

Glaucon continues after this analogy to fortify the worth of injustice by supposing a case of a perfectly unjust person who appears to all others as entirely just, and a perfectly just person who appears to all others as entirely unjust (Plato 2.360e – 361d). However, the context of the analogy regarding the Ring of Gyges is sufficient to illustrate man's inherent selfish nature.

What is truly important to recognize is where Socrates interrupts Glaucon's account for injustice. He only interrupts after the supposition of perfectly just and unjust persons who suffer harm and reap rewards respectively; Socrates does not cut in to object following the Ring of Gyges analogy. In fact, Socrates remains silent for most of Glaucon's account, interrupting only once to briefly exclaim how extravagant Glaucon's argument is (Plato 2.361d). Socrates, who appears very likely to point out any slip in another's argument, passes by this implication of selfishness. He does not immediately refute Glaucon's claim that both the just and unjust persons would act the same if free of fearful consequence or retribution, thereby, he offers a silent concession to its truth.

Moreover, Socrates later buys into the notion of man's selfishness as the basis of their ideal state. He concedes with Glaucon's earlier observations, stating that "... a state comes into existence because no individual is self-sufficing... if one man gives another what he has to give in exchange for what he can get, it is because each finds to do so is

92

for his own advantage" (Plato 2.369b – 369c). This sounds very reminiscent of the accepted compromise of justice that Glaucon had already mentioned (Plato 2.359b). Once again, the foundations of these precepts are that people are essentially selfish. Furthermore, the notion that morality is a social construct to constrain selfish human nature is a powerful and plausible premise later elaborated by philosophers ranging from Thomas Hobbes to Friedrich Nietzsche (Brenzel 156).

The corporation can be seen as the epitome of selfishness in the modern industrialized world. Certainly, the behaviour of the corporation best resembles the position put forth by Thrasymachus and Glaucon. It is a legally protected entity which bears the sole purpose of maximizing profit and it defends its participants by severing social accountability for any wrongdoings. Mark Achbar, Jennifer Abbott, and Joel Bakan's documentary film, *The Corporation*, brings together academic and industry experts to explore the moral (or, rather, amoral) nature of the corporation as an institution. The modern history of the corporation is collaboratively explained by numerous experts. Noam Chomsky, Institute Professor at MIT, explains that the corporation developed as a dominant institution over the past century, and that they were "originally associations of people chartered by a state to perform some particular function, like a group of people who want to build a bridge over the Charles River" (Achbar 00:08:40). Mary Zepernick, co-founder of Program on Corporations, Law and Democracy, elaborates further with the following:

> There were very few chartered corporations in early United States history. And, the ones that existed had clear stipulations in their state-issued charters – how long they could operate, the amount of capitalization, what they made, or did, or maintained, a turnpike or whatever – it was in their charter. And, they didn't do anything else. They didn't own, or couldn't own, another corporation. Their shareholders were liable, and so on. (Achbar 00:09:00)

93

The original form of the corporation was substantially different from today's corporation. Howard Zinn, author of *A People's History of the United States*, explains that corporations acquire more legal freedom with the implementation of the Fourteenth Amendment at the conclusion of the Civil War, a constitutional law intended to give equal rights to newly freed slaves, which is twisted by corporate lawyers who convince the U.S. Supreme Court that corporations are legal persons (Achbar 00:10:30). Chomsky elaborates on Zinn's account by adding the following:

> Corporations were given the rights of mortal persons, but then special kinds of persons, persons who have no moral conscience. These are a special kind of persons which are designed by law to be concerned only for their stockholders, and not say for what are sometimes called their stakeholders, like the community, or the workforce. (Achbar 00:13:40)

However, since a corporation is not in actuality a living, thinking person, we must recognize that the actions taken by a corporation are made manifest by the decisions and actions of its constituent members. The most grotesque aspect of the corporation is that the institution itself explicitly dictates to the constituent members that they must prioritize the profitability of the corporation over all and any other conflicting factors. Furthermore, in order to facilitate the process of morally unconcerned profitability, the corporation provides its constituents – the stockholders, executive members, decision makers, and employees – with limited liability, a severance of each individual constituent's accountability to society. The corporation as an institution acts as a lubricant encouraging those who participate in its system to act as cold, calculating profitability machines, where destruction is an allowable side effect.

To demonstrate the selfish behaviour of the corporation, recall the Nike sweatshop fiasco which unfolded in the media and the courts from the late 1990s to the early 2000s. Kristen Bell DeTienne and Lee W. Lewis' article, "The Pragmatic and

Ethical Barriers to Corporate Social Responsibility Disclosure: The Nike Case,"

objectively reviews the details surrounding this case study. DeTienne and Lewis explain

that companies engaging in public dialogue inevitably encounter the problem of "how to

ethically, legally, and effectively disclose information while maintaining a positive image

(DeTeinne 359). Since the corporation's primary concern is profitability and its public

image is directly related to maintaining revenue, that Nike must protect its appearance of

good character is of utmost importance, while expressing the truth is a secondary,

expendable objective. In *The Corporation*, Robert Monks, a corporate governance

advisor, claims that:

> Again and again, we have the problem that whether [a business obeys] the law or not is a
> matter of whether it is cost effective. If the chance of getting caught and the penalty are
> less than the cost to comply [with the law], people think of it as being just a business
> decision. (Achbar 00:38:30)

In order to protect its public image, and its profitability, accordingly, Nike did not

disclose the unfair working conditions discovered during the corporation's own self

evaluation (DeTienne 364). In order to defend hiding this information from investors and

the public, Nike plead that they were protected under the First Amendment and, as free

speech, the truthfulness of statements in question is immaterial (DeTienne 365). In

effect, Nike was trying to separate itself from accountability. Their argument attempts to

establish a precedent where businesses are not liable for making false claims.[24] It is

important to reflect upon the great effort the corporation will take to protect its profits.

Notice that Nike does not even confront the issue on the basis of using sweatshops may

be unethical business practice. That issue is placed to the side by Nike. Instead, they

twist the hearings to focus on what a business can and cannot get away with saying. Nike

---

[24] At one point during the lengthy court procedures, Justice Joyce Kennard of the California Supreme Court
ruled that businesses are obligated to speak truthfully (DeTienne 366); however, due to appeals and an out-
of-court settlement, the issue has never truly been resolved by the U.S. legal system (DeTienne 370).

shifts the focus of the debate in order to better determine the extent of a corporations'

accountability to the public. In doing so, Nike is also pushing for more freedoms for the

corporation, as if limited liability was not more than enough.

In a manner of speaking, the corporation's limited liability acts as a Ring of

Gyges for many of today's businessmen. In the Nike case, it was neither the executive

members of the board, nor the stockholders, nor the regional managers who were held in

fault for allowing the use of sweatshop labour in the manufacturing of their products;

rather, it was the corporation itself which was brought into the legal proceedings.

Effectively, the legal rights of the corporation have severed accountability for the people

responsible for contracting labour out to the sweatshop. This is the circumstance for

many corporate crimes. Even if the corporation is found guilty of a crime, they are

merely levied a fine, no one is likely incarcerated for the corporate crime, and business

carries on as usual. In this way, the corporation acts for modern businessmen exactly as

the Ring did for Gyges – neither must be concerned for any fearful consequences or

retribution. It is this lack of accountability that leads Robert Hare, FBI consultant on

psychopaths, to the following:

> If we look at a corporation as a legal person, it may not be that difficult to actually draw
> the transition between psychopathy in the individual to psychopathy in the corporation.
> We can go through the characteristics that define this particular disorder one by one and
> see how they apply to corporations. [Corporations] would have all the characteristics.
> And, in fact, in many respects, a corporation of that sort is the prototypical psychopath.
> (Achbar 00:42:00)

Since the constituents of the corporation have little to fear with regards to retribution,

they become free to act callously, with no concern for the impact of their actions on

others. As Glaucon has put forward in Plato's *Republic*, moved by greed, people will

desire to do wrong, while seeking to avoid harm brought upon oneself (Plato 2.358e).

This is exactly the condition established by the legal status of the corporation; hence it is the Ring of Gyges for the modern business community.

However, now that we have considered people's propensity towards selfishness, we must shift focus from this harsh view of humanity to reflect upon the exceptional character exhibited by superheroes. Here, we will consider both Iron Man and Batman. Since these superheroes' great power is derived from an abundance of wealth, intellect, and technology, it ought to be easier to relate to their motives rather than the motives of a nearly omnipotent superhero, such as Superman. Additionally, both Bruce Wayne and Tony Stark are the primary owners and decision makers for massive, transnational corporations, Wayne Enterprises and Stark Industries, respectively. Although these two characters are so closely tied to corporations, which we have associated with selfishness and denying social accountability, both characters exhibit an exceptional code of ethical conduct which leads them to live as superheroes. The films *Iron Man* and *Batman Begins* both depict the origins of these superheroes and, as such, bear witness to the characters' transition from typical selfish billionaires to morally responsible superheroes.

Jon Favreau's *Iron Man* depicts the origins of the Marvel superhero of the same name. Tony Stark has lived a life of incredible privilege as the brilliant heir to Stark Industries, a corporation which specializes in robotics and weapons manufacturing. Early on, the film presents a montage showing Stark as a child genius and his various technological and business achievements culminating in his current position as CEO of Stark Industries (Favreau 00:04:15). As expected, Stark exhibits the character traits one would expect of someone so rich and privileged – he is aloof, a gambler, a womanizer, he could care less about formalities, and he is so rich he can pretty much do whatever he pleases (Favreau 00:06:25). However, we are also confronted with the events that will change Stark's perspective on the world early in the film. The very introduction of the film presents the impetus of Stark's life, when he becomes the victim of his own weaponry while in Afghanistan for a demonstration of his latest missile (Favreau 00:02:30). Shortly after suffering his near fatal injury, Stark witnesses first hand that his company's weapons are being used by terrorists (Favreau 00:20:45). Another brilliant hostage of the terrorists saves Tony Stark's life by constructing an improvised pacemaker of sorts, which will keep the shrapnel in his heart from killing him. From suffering the effects of his merchandise personally, Stark realizes the damage he has helped inflict upon the world, and these experiences incite his paradigm shift. After escaping the terrorists using the first Iron Man armour, Stark returns to the United States and announces that Stark Industries will cease all arms manufacturing. Additionally, he admits "I have become comfortable with a system that has zero accountability" (Favreau 00:44:30). Although Stark has acknowledged the error of his ways, attempting to make amends, he is told that his decision to pull out of the arms market may not be in the best interests of Stark Industries, and the board of directors may take action otherwise (Favreau 00:58:00). Later, he discovers that his company is dealing arms illicitly to terrorists, and he resolves to take action against this, exclaiming:

> They've been dealing under the table, and I'm going to stop them. I'm going to find my weapons, and destroy them. (Favreau 01:28:10)

In order to persuade his assistant and confidant, Pepper Potts, that his superheroic intentions are not foolishness, he adds the following:

> I'm not crazy, Pepper. I just finally know what I have to do. And, I know in my heart that it's right. (Favreau 01:29:10)

Note the added meaning here, since there remains shrapnel in Stark's heart from the Stark Industries bomb that nearly killed him. That Stark feels his obligation to correct the wrongs he has helped to bring into the world is both figurative and literal. Reflecting upon this narrative, it seems that Tony Stark picks up the mantle of Iron Man as a means of alleviating the guilt he feels for the destruction and suffering his company's weapons have caused.

The story of Bruce Wayne's transformation into Batman is substantially different than that of Tony Stark's transformation into Iron Man, although the two remain similar. Christopher Nolan's film, *Batman Begins*, depicts the origins of Batman and Bruce Wayne's paradigm shift. Bruce Wayne, like Tony Stark, is the heir to a billion dollar corporation; however Wayne Enterprises does not deal exclusively in manufacturing weaponry. Bruce Wayne has a life of incredible privilege like Tony Stark, yet his is tragically stained at a young age when he witnesses the brutal killing of his parents by the desperate mugger, Joe Chill (Nolan 00:13:30). When young Bruce Wayne is told that Joe Chill has been apprehended, this is no consolation to a young boy who has just witnessed his parents murder (Nolan 00:15:30). For much of his lifetime, Bruce Wayne is consumed by anger and seeks only to deal swift vengeance upon Joe Chill for his crime. Although he is denied his revenge when Chill is killed by a mob henchmen (Nolan 00:25:40), he feels he must still do something. Between his best friend's condemnation of his desire for revenge (Nolan 00:27:25) and a criminal overlord's words of disgust (00:29:30), Bruce Wayne realizes he must first leave his life of privilege and become aware of the suffering in the world, before he can find the justice he seeks. Together, these events bring about the paradigm shift from rich boy to exceptional hero for Bruce

Wayne. Through years of traveling and training, Bruce Wayne hones his skills and his vision for justice to become the Batman we are familiar with today, the Dark Knight, the Caped Crusader. As Batman, Bruce Wayne has become a stalwart, unwavering beacon of justice. At the conclusion of *Batman Begins*, Batman remarks both that justice is more than simply revenge (Nolan 02:06:30) and that he will never need any thanks for his service to the people of Gotham (Nolan 02:10:45). Batman stands as a paragon of justice in Gotham.

Permit a quick contrast between the virtuous characters of Batman and Iron Man. Although both are superheroes, it might be argued that Batman is more of a superhero than Iron Man. In *Iron Man*, Tony Stark exhibits some character traits that are less than noble, even after his newfound sense of responsibility takes a hold of him. This is faithful to the mythos of the character developed in the Marvel comics, as well. In fact, in the comics series, Tony Stark was an alcoholic for quite some time, even piloting the Iron Man armour while under the influence. Such character traits are less than perfect, but through it all, Tony Stark maintained the desire to serve the public good, whether he was fully capable of achieving that end or not. Batman, however, has shown far fewer character flaws throughout his mythos and Nolan's film. Perhaps this can be explained by the nature of each character's paradigm shift. Since Bruce Wayne's paradigm shift was initiated by a crime against him, this honed his mission to fight crime to a strict ideal, whereas Tony Stark was inspired to turn to heroics from a sense of guilt from manufacturing weapons. In any case, it would not be fair to diminish Iron Man's superheroness because his motives stem from guilt instead of ideals. Both Iron Man and

Batman fight crime in the same capacity, with an altruistic sense of duty to the public and to serving justice.

Neither Tony Stark nor Bruce Wayne have a legally binding contract to serve the public good, nor do either character owe any particularly large debt to society, and yet they both serve their communities by trying to uphold peace and justice at great risk to themselves. They both have the power to fight injustice derived from an abundance of wealth, intellect, and technology, which they have at least partially gained from their close ties to their families' corporations. However, they have not succumbed to the selfishness the corporation easily provides them with. Instead, they employ their gifts in service of the public good. Both of these characters, while exaggerated, reflect real possibilities. Tony Stark and Bruce Wayne both experienced epiphanies which led to the characters' recognition of their duty to serve the public good. Perhaps their pivotal insights could be seen as exaggerations of real turning points in which people become aware of their obligation to the world around them. For instance, consider the testimony of Ray Anderson, CEO of Interface, the world's largest commercial carpet manufacturer:

> It dawned on me that the way I've been running Interface is the way of the plunderer, plundering something that's not mine, something that belongs to every creature on Earth. And, I said to myself, 'My goodness! The day must come when this is illegal – that when plundering is not allowed. I mean, it must come!' So, I said to myself, 'My goodness! Someday, people like me will end up in jail.' (Achbar 00:55:15)

Although Anderson's paradigm shift comes from the realization that he may be held accountable for his environmentally plundering business practices, regardless, he is prompted to begin serving the public good by making carpets sustainably. Although Anderson is in a position where he is protected by the institution of the corporation, he recognizes that the legacy of diminishment upon the environment left by industry is clearly wrong (Achbar 00:41:15). This is comparable to Tony Stark's realization that the

101

weapons manufactured by Stark Industries are being misused. Thus, Anderson is moved to reconcile his own guilt, much as Tony Stark was moved. Furthermore, Jeff Brenzel writes in his essay "Why Are Superheroes Good?" the following:

> In the case of superheroes, it's important to see that no matter how extensive their powers might be, they do not and cannot escape the very same questions about their potential for excellence that we must ask [ourselves]. That is, they have to ask themselves what sort and manner of person they are, and what is the best kind of life available for that sort of person to lead. (Brenzel 158-159)

The superhero narrative can be seen as an exaggerated narrative reflecting the choices we must make in our own lives. As such, they are given exceptional characteristics so that we might hope to live up to a fraction of the good that they do in their worlds. Brenzel further claims that we are most interested by superheroes because they are such exceptionally good characters – because they can resist the temptation of the Ring of Gyges (Brenzel 156). We see this resistance in the heroic acts in Batman and Iron Man narratives, and in the real world by the actions of people such as Ray Anderson. Such superhero narratives provide us with a noble example, however exaggerated it may be, of what it might be like to live life justly.

The hero of any tale is an exceptional character in some manner. Many superheroes qualify as exceptional immediately based upon their fantastic powers. This is not so with Iron Man and Batman, two individuals who have found the means to fight injustice through the freedom provided them by great wealth. However, at the foundation of the traditional superhero persona is a deeply rooted inclination towards acting justly. Thus, the superhero often acts contra typical selfish desires, upholding an uncompromising responsibility and duty to society. Bruce Wayne and Tony Stark are prime examples of resisting the temptation that is afforded by great power.

Defending the Imperfect Utopia

My encounters with academic writings on utopia have left me largely unsatisfied. It appears that much of the utopian scholarship fails to fully appreciate how utopian thought is represented in contemporary North American popular culture. Instead, it seems that many utopian scholars prefer to restrict their studies of utopia to its namesake literary genre. Such a restriction entails an ignorance of the pervasiveness of utopian thought in contemporary culture by and large. In order to help facilitate a fuller appreciation of how utopia is represented in contemporary North American popular culture, I apply my analysis of utopia to Alan Moore's *Watchmen*, a groundbreaking comic book series from 1986-87, collected into a graphic novel, which is presently being made into a film by director Zack Snyder. An analysis of utopia in *Watchmen* exemplifies three fundamental forms of utopia; Ozymandias' attempt to establish a unified utopia; Dr. Manhattan's attempt to create an isolated utopia; and, Rorschach's attempt to maintain the status quo as utopia. The most intriguing of the three forms of utopia is the status quo utopia, which is the more frequently portrayed form in North American popular culture. Through an analysis of utopia in *Watchmen* I argue that the realm of utopian scholarship must be expanded to encompass a study of romanticizing the current cultural condition.

Before proceeding to analyze *Watchmen*, any utopian discourse ought to clearly establish how the terms will be used. The term *utopia* has developed a diverse set of associations which makes discourse on the subject prone to miscommunication. As such, to participate in the utopian discourse, one must first clarify exactly how the terminology will be employed. Hence, I contextualize my use of certain terms within the context of ideas presented by Gregory Claeys and Lyman Tower Sargent in *The Utopia Reader* and Frederic Jameson in *Archaeologies of the Future*.

Here, the term utopia, more or less, denotes a society of satisfied individuals. One of the goals of this essay is to flesh out the meaning of utopia more thoroughly; thus, a simple and basic account is sufficient for the moment. Claeys and Sargent claim that when Thomas More coined the term utopia, he was making a pun of the Greek words *outopia* and *eutopia* (Claeys & Sargent 1). They further explain that, in Greek, *outopia* roughly meant no-place, while *eutopia* meant good-place (Claeys & Sargent 1). Although some utopian scholars uphold the significance of this double meaning, I argue that it is obsolete. Claeys and Sargent hold that "the primary characteristic of the utopia is its non-existence" (Claeys & Sargent 1). As such, the authors focus mainly on utopian thoughts as texts. Although they declare that utopian thought is not restricted to fiction, that it also pertains to constitutional and visionary texts (Claeys & Sargent 1), they do not seem to appreciate that there is an underlying desire to realise utopian desires in the real world.

Jameson, however, appears to accept the possibility of actualizing utopia in the world. While Claeys and Sargent simply refer to "social dreaming" when they use the term utopianism (Claeys & Sargent 1), Jameson sees a bifurcation between the utopian program and utopian impulse – respectively, the overt implementation of a utopian system and the covert expression and practice of utopian desires (Jameson 3). Thus, under the umbrella term, utopianism, there exists both conscious and unconscious attempts to realize utopian desires. While Claeys and Sargent's utopianism extends only so far as unrealized intentions, Jameson's program and impulse can become manifest in the world. This is an important distinction, since it demarcates Claeys and Sargent's focus on utopia as a literary genre and shows how Jameson allows utopian thought to enter into cultural analysis.

To further the position that we should eschew notions of *outopia* in utopian scholarship, consider the following argument. Certainly, Christianity's Eden and the world described in Aldous Huxley's *Brave New World* are utopias which invoke the notions of both *eutopia* and *outopia*. Such societies portray a satisfied populace and they do not exist in the real world. However, simply because there are examples of utopias that appear as good-places and no-places, it does not entail that both qualities are necessary for a society to be considered a utopia. Rather, the only necessary criterion for a utopia is that it qualifies as a *eutopia*. Here, the distinction between Claeys and Sargent's utopianism and Jameson's utopian impulse and utopian program is made clear. The social dreaming of utopianism is most comfortable within the realm of literature, while the utopian impulse and program can both become actualized. Christian monastic movements and Robert Owen's New Lanark Mills immediately come to mind when one reflects upon attempts to establish utopias in the real world. These attempts to establish real utopian communities go beyond mere "social dreaming." The implementation of these utopian programs is sufficient to refute that *outopia* is an essential characteristic of utopia. In light of this, I employ the term utopia, not to necessarily imply any sense of non-existence, but primarily to denote the good-place. Although Moore's *Watchmen* is a work of fiction, this analysis remains concerned with utopia as the good-place, rather than examining the significance of its non-existence. By eschewing *outopia*, a utopian analysis is less likely to be detached from its cultural import. Accordingly, we must keep

105

in mind how the narrative reflects various ideologies in contemporary North American popular culture.

Now, as we turn our focus towards *Watchmen*, contextualizing the text within the superhero genre and synopsising the plot of the narrative are indispensable to the analysis. First, Moore's *Watchmen* was one of three revolutionary texts for comics and graphic novels.[25] The text challenged many of the typical superhero tropes considered standard for the genre. Furthermore, Moore's characters operate with multiple layers of pastiche. For instance, Nite Owl is lifted from Blue Beetle, who in turn has been cloned from Batman. Accordingly, the characters in *Watchmen* speak to the audience as indirect representations of familiar superhero archetypes. Since *Watchmen* was published by DC Comics, this allowed Moore to freely work with obvious clones of major DC Comics characters, while simultaneously maintaining complete distance from directly affecting those characters' continuity. Moore's narrative operates on many complex levels, commenting on everything from the absurdities of the superhero genre to sexuality and gender. Jamie A. Hughes explains that the setting of *Watchmen* is atypically realistic for superhero comics of that era. In "'Who Watches the Watchmen?': Ideology and 'Real World' Superheroes," Hughes claims that *Watchmen* is set in a slightly altered version of the real world of 1985, where Richard Nixon is still President, and "superheroes are as common as they are in a place like Metropolis" (Hughes 548). By adding this degree of realism to a superhero narrative, Moore has injected a more poignant degree of cultural reflection into his tale.

---

[25] The other two revolutionary texts for the medium are Frank Miller's *Dark Knight Returns* and Art Spiegelman's *Maus*. These three texts are generally seen to have brought a sense of maturity to the content of the comics medium overall.

The characters of primary concern in this analysis of utopia are Ozymandias, Dr. Manhattan, and Rorschach. Ozymandias, a.k.a. Adrian Veidt, has no superpowers per se, however he has perfected his mental and physical attributes through sheer determination and force of will (Hughes 552).[26] It is Ozymandias' machinations to bring about a unified world free of Cold War tensions that provides the impetus for the narrative. Dr. Manhattan, a.k.a. Jon Osterman, is the only character in the story that has superpowers, which he gained through the typical nuclear accident (Hughes 552-553). His near omnipotence fosters a detachment from humanity, and it follows that his attempt at utopia is completely isolated from the world. Rorschach, a.k.a. Walter Joseph Kovacs, has absolutely no claim to any superpowers; "however, his vigilante methods are undeniably more stringent than the rest of his compatriots'" (Hughes 551). Rorschach is a conspiracy theorist and brutal detective. In the face of Ozymandias' utopia, Rorschach is adamant about maintaining the status quo.

Further, the crux of the utopian plot in *Watchmen* needs to be clarified. Matthew Wolf-Meyer's article "The World Ozymandias Made: Utopias in the Superhero Comic, Subculture, and the Conservation of Difference" offers a straightforward summary of the core of the narrative:

> [Ozymandias] sacrifices the lives of millions of New Yorkers in the face of an escalating Cold War in an attempt to affect a solidification of humanity in the face of such tragedy. The other heroes [namely, Rorschach, Nite Owl, and Silk Spectre] become embroiled in the utopian plot as [Ozymandias], in order to secure his plan, assassinates The Comedian; Rorschach begins an investigation, which then involves the other heroes, ending in the confrontation of [Ozymandias] and his plan by the other heroes. (Wolf-Meyer 508)

However, the story begins with the death of The Comedian and Rorschach's resulting investigation. It is not until the penultimate chapter that Ozymandias' plot for uniting the

---

[26] Although in this aspect Ozymandias may appear to be a clone of Batman, this is at most a partial pastiche. Nite Owl remains the more direct pastiche of Batman in *Watchmen*.

world is obliquely revealed to the reader. Although it is quite complicated, suffice it to say that Ozymandias' plot, basically, is to teleport a gigantic, genetically engineered, psychic "alien" into the middle of New York that will explode upon arrival, then releasing a horrific psychic impulse that will instantly kill millions of New Yorkers and traumatize hundreds of millions around the world. This manufactured threat of an alien invasion Ozymandias is sure will bring a cessation of hostilities between the Cold War superpowers and unite the nations of the world. When Dr. Manhattan and Rorschach learn the truth of this plot after it has already been enacted, Rorschach dissents and is killed by Dr. Manhattan to uphold the lie to the public, but then Dr. Manhattan departs the world and all its earthly affairs to create new life on Mars. Although the final chapters of *Watchmen* are quite fantastical, working through the various forms of utopia represented here helps facilitate an insight on utopia as it is represented broadly across contemporary North American popular culture.

Ozymandias' attempt to bring about a unified utopia is the most traditional form of utopia portrayed in *Watchmen*. As Ozymandias explains himself to Rorschach and Nite Owl in Chapter XI, he claims that after John F. Kennedy's assassination he reached a certain insight on the true state of affairs. He explains as follows:

> We all realized then how bad things were. I continued adventuring, but it seemed hollow. I fought only the symptoms, leaving the disease itself unchecked. I despised myself; my sham crusade. Knowing mankind's problems, I'd blinded myself to them. I felt helpless against forces greater than any I'd anticipated. (Moore XI, 19)

Here, Ozymandias explains his discontent with typical superhero crime-fighting. This prompts him to step back and devise a method to affect change on a larger scale. In the face of a growing nuclear threat, Ozymandias' rationale leads him to develop the alien plot to bring about a unified world. He later exclaims to the other heroes that, although he was "unable to unite the world by conquest... Alexander [the Great]'s method... I would trick it; frighten it towards salvation with history's greatest practical joke" (Moore XI, 24). The lie that Ozymandias must propagate to maintain his unified utopia is similar to the noble lie in Plato's *Republic*, insofar as they are both mass lies told to the populace in order to maintain the ideal society. Within the world of *Watchmen*, in the terms of utopian discourse, Ozymandias has taken his social dreams of utopia and brought them to fruition by implementing his utopian program. Wolf-Meyer characterizes Ozymandias' actions as a struggle for humanity's sake and an attempt "to make the world a better place for those less rich and powerful" (Wolf-Meyer 507). However, there is no evidence in the text that Ozymandias' utopia will usurp capitalism, nor is there any mention that it will make any attempt to instate socialist reform or policies. Rather, given Ozymandias background in business and economics, it would appear that the new unified utopia will continue along in the capitalist tradition. Furthermore, Ozymandias only claims that his new world will bring an end to war (Moore XI, 24). Hughes explains that Ozymandias changes the public's mindset from an "Us vs. Them" dyad to "One World, One Accord," which is seen on posters in numerous panels in the last chapter (Hughes 554). However, it should be noted that the "Us vs. Them" dyad would still function in Ozymandias unified utopia. The only difference is that the initial Us was one nation, the United States of America, opposing Them, the Soviet Union, while the latter Us encompasses the world as a whole, opposing a non-existent Them, the imaginary alien invaders. The scope and boundaries which determine the Us group has simply been expanded, and the opposing Them has shifted from the Soviets to the alleged alien threat. The real social change in Ozymandias' unified utopia is not found in a radical change of social structures; rather,

109

his utopia merely changes the dynamics of conflict, eliminating mass violence amongst peoples. Instead of a utopia based upon North American national identity, Ozymandias establishes a utopia based upon an ideology of a world identity as opposed to the fabricated ideals of the imaginary alien invaders.

That Dr. Manhattan wishes to create his own utopia is only briefly hinted in *Watchmen*, however it deserves some coverage here. Dr. Manhattan's ideas for utopia do not come into conflict with Ozymandias' utopian program or Rorschach's utopian impulse. In the narrative, we see how Dr. Manhattan's utopian impulses flourish into the makings of a utopian program. In Chapter IV, Dr. Manhattan leaves Earth for Mars due to a scandal in which the public is led to believe that he emits radiation that causes cancer, a hoax which was necessary in Ozymandias' plot to bring about utopia on Earth. Yet, once Dr. Manhattan is left alone on Mars, he begins to construct a marvellous city. Later, in Chapter IX, Dr. Manhattan discovers a renewed fascination for life's miracles, claiming they are "events with odds against so astronomical they're effectively impossible, like oxygen spontaneously becoming gold" (Moore IX, 26). Once the narrative has passed its climax, Dr. Manhattan expresses to Ozymandias his desire to create life (Moore XII, 27). What is interesting about Dr. Manhattan's utopian impulse is that it is rooted in a detachment from humanity. His near limitless powers have so detached him from humanity that he confesses in Chapter IV that with regards to fighting crime "the morality of my activities escapes me" (Moore IV, 14). Presumably, Dr. Manhattan's isolated utopia which he plans to create on Mars will be based on rationality. Since his utopia is free from humanity, per se, we are left to speculate whether it will be a perfect society. Many traditional utopian scholars might tend to agree with this premise.

In describing the Stalinist utopia, Jameson explains that utopia is "the ideal purity of a perfect [political] system that always had to be imposed by force on its imperfect and reluctant subjects" (Jameson xi). Here, Jameson succinctly describes the common preconception that utopias are perfect in political theory and only fail because of the diversity of ideologies amongst the populace. Hence, with Dr. Manhattan's guiding intellect and the removal of humanity, traditional utopia scholars may look quite favourably upon this isolated utopia. Even in isolation, the "Us vs. Them" dyad still operates on a less aggressive level. For one of Dr. Manhattan's founding principles is to establish a new form of life which is deliberately not human.

Nevertheless, the most intriguing representation of utopian thought in *Watchmen* resides in Rorschach's utopian impulse. According to Hughes, Rorschach shares a similar perception of the world with Ozymandias, since they both recognize that "society has problems that desperately need correction" (Hughes 551). However, Hughes explains further that "aside from his attempts to act as judge and jury for the criminals he captures, [Rorschach] can do little to stop the larger pattern of problems he sees" (Hughes 552). This inability to make broad strokes to affect change has two significant results at the conclusion of *Watchmen*. First, when Rorschach decides to expose the truth of Ozymandias' plot to the world, his lack of outright power brings about his murder to ensure his silence. Second, his investigative foresight led him to submit his journal to a newspaper publication, and the last panel of the narrative leads the reader to assume that Rorschach succeeds in revealing Ozymandias' sinister machinations posthumously, exposing the noble lie and disrupting the unified utopia. Wolf-Meyer characterizes Rorschach's position as a defence of "the dystopian status quo in the name of 'justice'"

111

(Wolf-Meyer 509). That characterization, however, is a misunderstanding of the nature of utopia. Every utopia is fundamentally derived from a particular ideology or set of beliefs. This means that utopias come in varying forms. The free market capitalist utopia is just as valid a form of utopia as the socialist utopia, the free love hippy utopia, the Christian monastic utopia, and so on. However, Wolf-Meyer is mistaken in aligning Rorschach's ideological utopia with the capitalist status quo. That is simply not the case. Rorschach dissents because of the horrendous methods used by Ozymandias to achieve utopia. This goes against his profound principles of right and justice. The utopian impulse which Rorschach seeks to defend is for a just utopia, not necessarily a capitalist utopia, although the two here coincide.

However, since Rorschach's attempt to maintain his just utopia coincides with a defence of the status quo, we find an entry point into a more common phenomenon in representations of utopia in contemporary North American popular culture. In *The Myth of the American Superhero*, John Shelton Lawrence and Robert Jewett put forth the proposition that there is a new archetypal plot formula found in North American popular narratives which operates as follows:

> A community in a harmonious paradise is threatened by evil; normal institutions fail to contend with this threat; a selfless superhero emerges to renounce temptations and carry out the redemptive task; aided by fate, his decisive victory restores the community to its paradisiacal condition.... (Lawrence & Jewett 6)

This new American monomyth – as Lawrence and Jewett phrase it – can be found in thousands of popular culture artefacts (Lawrence & Jewett 6). Once we are aware of the American monomyth it becomes readily apparent in narratives such as *JFK*, *The Matrix*, *The X-Files*, *Touched by an Angel*, and the *Star Trek*, *Star Wars*, *Rambo*, and *Die Hard* franchises, just to name a few examples. Quite frequently in these narratives, the utopia in question is simply the Western capitalist model, perhaps with some slight modification, such as the realistic setting of *Watchmen* including superheroes in the populace. Essentially, the American monomyth romanticizes the current cultural condition, rendering it the equivalent of utopia in its representation in popular narratives. Although the capitalist, liberal democracy remains an imperfect social system, it is rendered a utopia as it is in relation to the Other, once again utilizing the "Us vs. Them" dynamic. For Rorschach, Ozymandias' proposed compromise of maintaining the lie to the world is incommensurable with his ideals of justice, which Rorschach holds is commensurable with maintaining the status quo. The hero of the American monomyth must redeem the utopia's paradisiacal condition because their ideological basis is superior to the opposing Other's ideological set. This mode of representing North American values in popular culture speaks volumes on the status of national identity, especially during trying times such as the McCarthy era, the Cold War, and the War on Terror.

Furthermore, it appears that Jameson, Claeys and Sargent recognize the utopian elements of North American culture, but they fail to appreciate the pervasiveness with which North America is portrayed in popular culture as a utopia, at least insofar as it is an imperfect system with a satisfied populace. Claeys and Sargent acknowledge that since the late eighteenth century North America has projected utopian promises of greater equality and social justice on a national scale (Claeys & Sargent 3). Further, Jameson concedes the following:

> ...that the historic alternatives to capitalism have been proven unviable and impossible, and that no other socio-economic system is conceivable, let alone practically available. (Jameson xii)

Despite such concessions, neither Jameson nor Claeys and Sargent recognize the North American capitalist culture as a full-fledged utopia in its representations in popular

113

culture. Nevertheless, the North American utopia is in accordance with the converse of Jameson's premise that "the more surely a given [utopia] asserts its radical difference from what currently is, to that very degree it becomes, not merely unrealizable [sic], but, what is worse, unimaginable" (Jameson xv). The converse, of course, is that the closer a utopia is to the current status quo, the more realisable it is. It just so happens that capitalism, equality, and social justice forms the backbone of North American culture and, so it follows, that the capitalist-democratic utopia is fully realisable in North America. Hence, North America is commonly portrayed as a utopia in popular narratives. Moreover, evidence to support that North America is a utopia is the immense numbers of people from less fortunate areas of the world who seek to immigrate to this land of fortune, freedom, and opportunity. Thus, North America is a utopia in relation to societies and cultures excluded from it, since outsiders so desire to become included in the utopia.

By recognizing the structure of the American monomyth, it becomes apparent that utopia is a pervasive force in contemporary North American popular culture. My analysis of utopia in Alan Moore's *Watchmen* should help facilitate a fuller appreciation of how utopia is represented in contemporary North American popular culture. This analysis of utopia in *Watchmen* exemplifies three fundamental forms of utopia – the unified utopia, the isolated utopia, and the status quo as utopia. Through Rorschach's attempt to defend his just utopia, we find an entry point into the American monomyth and its correlative linking of national identity and utopian thought. This analysis of utopia in *Watchmen* makes the case that the realm of utopian scholarship must be expanded to encompass a study of romanticizing the current cultural condition.

Marvel Comics' *Civil War* as a Post-9/11 Text

The debate of security versus civil liberties has not let up since the events of 9/11. The current War on Terror is reinstating elements of paranoia that were persistent during the Cold War era. This paranoia is made manifest in policies that claim to increase national security while sacrificing civil liberties. Such limitations on liberties are evident in the implementation of the U.S. Patriot Act. The debate on the effectiveness of sacrificing civil liberties in maintaining security is prevalent today in the post-9/11 social climate. This debate's issues are reflected in film and literature, and Marvel Comics' most recent crossover event, *Civil War*, interrogates both Leftist and Rightist perspectives on the matters of prioritizing security over civil liberties. However, in a genre where superheroes function as moral beacons, this post-9/11 dilemma challenges that traditional role. The dilemma of choosing security or liberty becomes a question of which is the morally right position to defend for Marvel's superheroes. Since Marvel Comics' superheroes are divided on such a major post-9/11 issue, this poses a challenge to the traditional role of the superhero as a moral beacon. Through a consideration of selected texts that contemplate the social and political environment of North America since the events of 9/11, I argue that the Super Human Registration Act in Marvel's *Civil War* is reminiscent of the U.S. Patriot Act, the sentiments expressed in *Civil War* reflect those of North Americans to the dilemma of sacrificing civil rights for security, and, finally, as Marvel's superheroes confront this dilemma, the function of the superhero as a moral beacon is not lost in post-9/11 literature.

With respect to the social and political environment, this paper will attempt to situate the question of security before civil liberty as a significant aspect of archetypal

115

literature in post-9/11 North America. The central texts of this paper are the Marvel Comics' serials *Civil War* and *Civil War: Front Line*. While there are other texts that significantly tie-in to the story of *Civil War*, the selected serials should suffice in illustrating that the text reflects public sentiments in post-9/11 North America. In establishing the context of post-9/11 North America this chapter will focus on Slavoj Zizek's *Welcome to the Desert of the Real* and Nancy V. Baker's "National Security versus Civil Liberties." Finally, C. Stephen Layman, C. Stephen Evans, Bronislaw Malinowski, and Joseph Campbell provide ample support in analyzing the function of the superhero narrative in North American culture. Together, these secondary texts provide a solid foundation for understanding how such moral dilemmas affect the role of the superhero in post-9/11 literature.

Before discussing how Marvel's recent crossover event reflects the debate between security and civil liberties, I ought to briefly summarize the *Civil War* and *Civil War: Front Line* serials. Every issue of the *Civil War* serial begins with a summary of the story. The following summary is found in *Civil War* #7, the concluding issue of the story:

> A Superhuman Registration Act has been passed which requires all individuals possessing paranormal abilities to register with the government. Those who do not register are considered criminals. Some heroes, such as Iron Man, see this as a natural evolution of the role of superhumans in society and a reasonable request. But Captain America has gathered an underground resistance movement against the new law. (*Civil War* #7 1)

Essentially, the premise of the story is set up in *Civil War* #1. The first issue of the serial details a young and reckless team of super heroes, the New Warriors, who unwittingly instigate a massacre in Stamford, Connecticut while they are fighting a group of super-powered criminals. The New Warriors know that these criminals are a little out of their

116

league, but their team leader, Speedball, insists they pursue the fight since it might increase the ratings of their reality show. The conflict ends as one of the criminals, Nitro, unleashes a massive explosion in a residential area. The death toll is approximately 600, and about 60 of those were school children. This tragedy becomes the last straw for public tolerance of superhuman misbehaviour, and legislation for the Superhuman Registration Act is passed swiftly through congress (*Civil War* #1 41). This law requires that every U.S. citizen with superpowers must register their identity with the government, or be considered an "unregistered combatant," and a criminal. The *Civil War* serial delivers the core of this story, while *Front Line* presents the perspective of two reporters who become deeply involved in events of the superhero civil war. This premise provides a scenario for some exciting storytelling for some of our favourite heroes. However, the tale of *Civil War* is not only entertaining; the narrative reflects events and concerns of post-9/11 North America.

The events of September 11th, 2001 were unquestionably tragic. The attacks on the World Trade Center and the Pentagon were atrocious and unthinkable. However, these events have been thrust into cultural unconscious with a vengeance. Slavoj Zizek recognizes this in his book *Welcome to the Desert of the Real*. He argues that, for most people, the destruction of the World Trade Center was a televised tragedy reminiscent of some spectacular catastrophe film (Zizek 11). As such, the tragedy of September 11th, 2001 has become a part of the collective experience of North Americans. Since the tragedy was so exhaustively covered in the media, it was unavoidable that 9/11 would become a landmark event. The attacks on 9/11 initiated George W. Bush's War on Terror, and it is the War on Terror that attracts my attention here. In the wake of the 9/11

117

attacks, North America has been defined by the war on terror and the debates spawned by hasty policy-making. Zizek further argues that we have entered an era of paranoia. In this era, terrorists publicly claim credit for their acts less frequently and even the so-called anti-terrorist measures are clouded in secrecy. For Zizek, all of this contributes to "an ideal breeding ground for conspiracy theories and generalized social paranoia" (Zizek 37). These are some of the sentiments that *Civil War* and *Front Line* confront.

In particular, the latter issues of *Front Line* portray two reporters who uncover the underlying conspiracy behind the events of civil war. They discover that Tony Stark (a.k.a. Iron Man) had manipulated events such that more superhumans would register with the government. Pursuing this goal, Stark committed the following acts and measures: manipulating the stock market to raise funds for a superhero pension plan; using government funds to build a secret, high-tech prison in another dimension; enlisting a cybernetic clone of Thor, the Norse god of thunder, to be an enforcer of registration; recruiting a large number of violent criminals, the Thunderbolts, to bolster pro-registration forces; and, finally, staging an assassination attempt on a foreign dignitary, bringing the U.S. to the brink of war with Atlantis. While the conspiracy exposed in *Front Line* is exaggerated, it can be seen as a caricature of Leftist conspiracy theory in North America. Here, we see that *Front Line* echoes some of the sentiments prevalent in North America. The BBC documentary *9/11: The Conspiracy Files* examines many factions and personages behind the so-called "9/11 truth" movement. While the documentary is largely biased in maintaining official accounts of the attacks on 9/11 and the film decidedly undercuts any validity in 9/11 truth theories, it nevertheless presents how widespread these attitudes are throughout the U.S. and, by implication, North

118

America and Europe, as well. The documentary recounts truth theories from Professor Jim Fetzer of Scholars for 9/11 Truth, Dylan Avery of Loose Change (an internet site dedicated to propagating 9/11 truth theories), and Alex Jones, a Texan radio talk show host. Each of these theorists maintains that there was strong government and military involvement in the 9/11 attacks and that those agencies are working furiously to cover up the truth. They uphold, more or less, that the real terrorists of 9/11 are the Bush administration, whom uses the threat of terrorist attacks as an excuse for global imperialism. These sentiments are reflected in the conspiracy revealed in *Front Line*. Like the 9/11 conspiracy theories, *Front Line* reveals that Iron Man, an agent of the government and registration, manufactures a situation to instil the threat of foreign attack in order to tighten domestic security and bolster the numbers of registered superhumans. This is the essential nature of the Green Goblin's assassination attempt against an Atlantean dignitary. Iron Man had staged this assassination attempt in order to manipulate public support and gain favour for pro-registration forces (*Front Line* #11 29).

In illustrating the parallels between Marvel Comics' *Civil War* and post-9/11 North America, Nancy V. Baker's article, "National Security versus Civil Liberties," provides us with a solid resource to consider the political and social context. Unlike the speculative nature of the conspiracy or "truth" theories involving the 9/11 attacks, the implementation and enforcement of measures enacted as a result of the attacks is much more observable and quantifiable. Thus, it can stand as more reliable evidence. As such, considering journalism of a more investigative nature provides a more credible backdrop in analyzing the parallels between post-9/11 North America and the events depicted in Marvel Comics' *Civil War* crossover event. Baker's article is a prime representation of

119

the post-9/11 dilemma of security or liberty. In general, Baker argues that civil liberties are categorized as luxuries during wartime; thus, they are expendable during the war effort (Baker 548). However, she also notes that the Bush administration takes civil liberties to be "gaping holes in the security fabric [that] must be sealed off permanently if the nation is to be safe" (Baker 548). In *Civil War*, the civil liberties of superhumans are sacrificed for the sake of security, as well. The implementation and enforcement of the Superhuman Registration Act places superheroes under extreme conditions. Those superheroes who wish to keep their identities secret are pursued relentlessly and, if they are apprehended, they are imprisoned indefinitely, without access to legal aide, unless they register in accordance with the Superhuman Registration Act. Further, like the Bush administration, the Superhuman Registration Act is meant to be a permanent solution. The increasing totalitarian measures of the government permeate the theme of *Civil War* and *Front Line*, but there seems to be a ground for these sentiments in actual U.S. policy and implementation. Following this line of thought, I will focus on two issues prevalent in post-9/11 North America and Marvel Comics' *Civil War* – privacy and due process.

It should be obvious that privacy is one of the main concerns of masked superheroes regarding the Superhuman Registration Act. Spider-Man initially makes the point that he conceals his identity in order to protect those close to him from those who would do them harm as a means to get to him (*Civil War* #1 26, *Front Line* #1 11-13). While the Superhuman Registration Act does not require that superheroes go public with their identities, it does require that the government have access to their true identity. However, in a world where super criminals could easily steal that information from the government, Spider-Man's concern remains valid. Spider-Man's case is particularly

120

interesting since he changes sides during the course of the superhero civil war. Early in *Civil War*, Spider-Man is convinced by his close friend, Iron Man, that registration is the right thing for superheroes to do. Following this, Spider-Man is further convinced to go public with his identity as a sign of good faith in the hopes that his actions would inspire anti-registration superheroes to register in accordance with the Superhuman Registration Act (*Civil War* #2 28-32). However, later in the series, Spider-Man can not reconcile his conscience with the use of the cybernetic Thor clone and imprisoning superheroes in the Negative Zone, so he resolves to leave the Avengers and cease assisting in the apprehension of unregistered superheroes (*Civil War* #5 6-11). While this relieves Spider-Man from any benefits the government may have provided him, his first concern is for those he loves, Mary Jane and Aunt May (*Civil War* #5 11). The interesting aspect here is that this will prove to be very problematic and tragic for Spider-Man. Not only do the government know his identity, but so does the public, including everyone Spider-Man has angered in the past. This allows Spider-Man's enemies to target his loved ones, just as he feared most.[27] This acts as a narrative convention in order to confirm the risks of a superhero revealing his or her identity. Another valid concern about privacy is made with Speedball in *Front Line* #2. Speedball is the only member of the New Warriors to survive the explosion at Stamford, and he is being held personally accountable for the tragedy. Since the explosion at Stamford, Speedball's powers have become sporadic, and most people assume that his powers have been nullified. For this reason, Speedball is incarcerated at an "undisclosed location" with non-powered inmates. While under this detention, a federal agent tries to bargain with him to register his identity under the

---

[27] It does not take long for criminals to capitalize on Spider-Man's exposed identity. Kingpin sends a sniper to his home, and one of his loved ones is put into a coma in *The Amazing Spider-Man* #538.

Superhuman Registration Act, regardless of any loss of powers, simply because his case is so high profile. However, the agent informs Speedball that his identity has already been disclosed to the press. Furthermore, when Speedball pleads to see his lawyer and complains that his rights are being violated, the agent responds with "You're an unregistered combatant... I define your rights" (*Front Line* #2 17). After Speedball's identity is disclosed to the public, he endures vicious attacks in prison from both guards and inmates. Speedball's case can be seen as the tip of the iceberg of potential hazards of superheroes disclosing their identities. Once again, Speedball's misfortune is a narrative convention that reinforces condemnation of the Superhuman Registration Act. In post-9/11 North America, however, privacy concerns are somewhat different, but they still share strong similarities. In the U.S., the implementation of the Patriot Act means that government agencies have much greater access to the personal information of U.S. citizens. For instance, Baker explains that Title II of the Patriot Act makes it far easier for the government to intercept communications, instigate searches, access personal records, conceal searches and background checks from those searched, and limit the liability of those who disclose this information to the government (Baker 560-561). While the conditions under which the government invades personal privacy in the real world differs from the invasion of privacy depicted in Marvel Comics' *Civil War*, both exhibit a strong desire by the administration to control identifying information. Moreover, in both cases the government acts in the interest of maintaining security.

The other major echo in *Civil War* of the post-9/11 war on terror is the secret prison for detaining superheroes, Number 42. This prison is in a massive institution designed to incarcerate super-powered individuals – primarily, unregistered superheroes.

Unregistered superheroes are held in this gulag indefinitely, unless they register in accordance with the Superhuman Registration Act. The Number 42 prison is a reflection of how suspected terrorists and material witnesses were detained following the 9/11 attacks. Baker claims that the first issue of denying due process emerged shortly after the attacks when the Justice Department's "preventive campaign of arrest and detention" detained approximately 1,200 foreign nationals "presumed to be security threats or material witnesses of such threats" (Baker 556). These detentions ranged in duration from a few days to 400 days, many were held under solitary confinement and 24-hour lighting, and many had difficulty contacting their families and attorneys (Baker 557). Furthermore, some of the detainees were denied petition for a writ of habeas corpus (Baker 558).[28] Again, the Patriot Act allows this behaviour. Here, we see many of the same conditions of post-9/11 U.S. reflected in *Civil War*. For instance, as has already been mentioned, Speedball's case throughout *Front Line* is a prime example illustrating how superheroes were denied due process under the Superhuman Registration Act. Speedball is held accountable for his late team-mates, as well as Nitro, the criminal who caused the explosion. The federal agent offers Speedball the chance to register and be forgiven of all accountability, or face incarceration "at the pleasure of the United States government" (*Front Line* #2 17). All of this occurs before Speedball has access to any legal counsel. Then, once legal aide is provided, Speedball's counsel is Jennifer Walters (a.k.a. She-Hulk), an advocate for registration and strong arm for the pro-registration forces (*Front Line* #3 13-20). Clearly, this exhibits a blatant conflict of interests where Ms. Walters could not possibly represent her client's best interests. Furthermore, it is not

---

[28] Habeas corpus is the right protected by the U.S. Constitution for a prisoner to appeal whether her/his detention is lawful or not (Baker 558).

only Speedball's circumstances which portray violations of prisoner's rights; the harsh conditions which unregistered combatants endure in Prison 42 are alluded to in *Front Line* #6. In a letter to his family, Speedball recounts the suffering of other imprisoned superheroes. He explains that they receive very little freedom to exercise, frequent solitary confinement, and the cumulative effect is too much for some superhumans who then commit suicide (*Front Line* #6 14-15). The conditions of unregistered superheroes bear a striking resemblance to the harsh treatment of foreign nationals shortly after the attacks on 9/11, and the effects of the Superhuman Registration Act continues to echo the implementation of the Patriot Act.

The security-civil liberty dilemma is a significant aspect of post-9/11 culture that is interpreted and interrogated through literature. Marvel's *Civil War* crossover event represents an ideal, archetypal text in reflecting the ethical perspectives of both Leftist and Rightist attitudes concerning this debate. However, while the line between right and wrong is not very clear on such a moral dilemma, the superhero narrative still functions as a moral beacon, reflecting the values of North American culture. The moral ambiguity of the debate between security and civil liberties challenges the superhero's role as a moral beacon since there is no immediately clear answer to which position is right. This challenge to the role of the superhero comes from the dynamic of the conflict. The conflict in *Civil War* does not pit superheroes against super villains in the usual sense. Actually, super villains do not play a central role in this tale at all, besides their forced compliance in aiding the pro-registration forces. Instead of this traditional binary opposition of clearly evil criminals being thwarted by heroes with good intentions, *Civil War* presents a tale of heroes divided on an issue where both sides have good intentions.

However, while both pro-registration and anti-registration forces make justified arguments to support their respective stances, the anti-registration heroes represent the more heroic stance. In order to defend this position, we must first briefly analyze the actions taken by heroes on each side of the debate. In "Why Be a Superhero? Why Be Moral?," C. Stephen Layman acknowledges that many superheroes act according to a sense of duty. He grants that this does seem like a simple mantra, but that some great philosophers defend this ethical account, such as Immanuel Kant and F. H. Bradley (Layman 199). Layman explicitly claims that some superheroes "must do the right thing because it's right, and not for some sort of self-interested reward" (Layman 199). The problem with this, as Layman realizes, is that acting according to what is right may not always be the rational thing to do; in other words, rationality does not necessarily coincide with morality (Layman 200). Furthermore, in "Why Should Superheroes Be Good?," C. Stephen Evans also supports this ethical code found in many superheroes. Evans also points out that other prominent philosophers, such as Soren Kirkegaard, maintain "not merely that it is a good thing to love our neighbours as ourselves, but that we have a duty to do so" (Evans 174). This type of ethical code characterizes Captain America in *Civil War*, and, by extension, the rest of the anti-registration forces in general. This adherence to duty is exemplified in Captain America's decision to oppose the Superhuman Registration Act. In *Civil War* #1, Captain America is ordered by government officials to lead the Avengers in rounding up any superheroes who refuse to register. Captain America emphatically refuses to assist in the arrest of "people who risk their lives for [their] country every day of the week" (*Civil War* #1 30). Captain America has no vested interest in protecting his identity – the government knows that he is Steve

Rogers since he is a soldier in the U. S. Army – yet, he still chooses to defend the identities of other superheroes. Captain America fights to protect the identities of superheroes based on the principle of the matter. Many may hold that going along with the pro-registration forces is the most reasonable response since it is in the interests of his own health and well-being, but Captain America must follow his soul, his duty. Another moment indicating Captain America's devotion to ideals comes at the conclusion of the crossover event in *Front Line* #11. This comes from reporter Sally Floyd who is interviewing Captain America after he had surrendered, effectively ceasing the superhero civil war.[29] Miss Floyd confronts Captain America claiming, "Your problem is that you're fighting for an ideal – it's all you know how to do" (*Front Line* #11 15). In addition, she goes on to say the following:

> America is no longer about mom and apple pie... it's about high cholesterol and Paris Hilton and scheming your way to the top... The country I love treats its celebrities like royalty and its teachers like dirt. (*Front Line* #11 15)

The point Miss Floyd makes is that Captain America is out of touch with the American public and, as such, he should realise that the people support the Superhuman Registration Act. However, it is obvious that Captain America's ideals occupy a moral high ground well above the characteristics that Sally Floyd attributes to America. Captain America's ideals uphold truth and justice, which are far nobler than the laziness, corruption, materialism, and ignorance that Sally Floyd characterizes as the sentiments of the majority of Americans. Furthermore, Miss Floyd's attitude represents the central flaw of democracy and utilitarianism.

---

[29] Many of the anti-registration superheroes gave up once Captain America surrendered. However, there are still factions of superheroes who have gone underground, like Spider-Man, Wolverine, and Dr. Strange. Others, like Storm and Black Panther, can afford to continue to oppose registration since they have diplomatic immunity as foreign dignitaries.

The flaw of democracy and utilitarianism is also found in Iron Man and his pro-registration supporters. This flaw is found in the neglect of the minority in both democracy and utilitarianism. Both of these ideologies favour the majority – for democracy, the majority rules, and with utilitarianism, whichever act benefits the majority is the best. The flaw here ought to be obvious. Both of these systems would permit any edict provided the majority supports it. Examples of this can be found in Nazi Germany or the Japanese internment camps in North America during World War II. Simply because an idea has the support of the majority does not determine its moral status. This is evident in the implementation of the Superhuman Registration Act in Marvel Comics' *Civil War*. In addition, *Front Line* makes a general comparison between the implementation of the Superhuman Registration Act and U.S. concentration camps (*Front Line* #1 30-32) and the U.S. war in Vietnam (*Front Line* #4 28-32). Nevertheless, we should consider Iron Man's role in this fascist ordeal more closely. As mentioned earlier, Iron Man is revealed as the mastermind behind many sinister schemes during the superhero civil war, yet he is not entirely heartless. Iron Man drifts far from the ethical codes of some superheroes, such as those to which Layman and Evans refer. Like a true utilitarian, Iron Man is focused entirely on consequences and results. Hence, Iron Man permits manipulating the stock market, building a super prison in another dimension, creating an artificial god of thunder, enlisting known violent criminals, and staging an assassination attempt on a foreign dignitary. However, Iron Man allows these underhanded means in hopes of arriving at a good end. Iron Man is trying to create the greatest amount of good for the greatest number of people. While that sounds like a noble cause, it is very difficult to reconcile his actions as morally sound. Even Iron Man

127

is depicted as feeling guilty for his actions. In *Front Line* #11, after Sally Floyd and Ben Urich confront him about his manipulation of events, Tony Stark has an emotional breakdown (*Front Line* #11 31-32). The concluding issue of *Front Line* reveals Iron Man's conspiracy, but it also reveals his remorse. This shows that while Iron Man has seen himself as working towards a greater good, he recognizes that the means he employed to get there were wrong. Iron Man's own sense of guilt confirms the lack of moral conviction in the fascistic and totalitarian measures used to implement the Superhuman Registration Act.

In order to fully appreciate the challenge this moral dilemma poses to the traditional role of the superhero, it is helpful to look at the superhero narrative as a mythical tale. Bronislaw Malinowski's charter theory of myth is particularly insightful in reflecting upon this challenge to the traditional role of the superhero. In "The Foundations of Faith and Morals," Malinowski argues that myth is essentially a charter of belief, ritual, and ethics (Malinowski 139). In addition, Malinowski claims in "Myth in Primitive Psychology" that "the function of myth... is to strengthen tradition and endow it with a greater value" (Malinowski 114). Malinowski acknowledges that myth functions, not only as a moral instructor, but in justifying specific institutions, as well. In his introduction to *Malinowski and the Work of Myth*, Ivan Strenski notes that, early in his career, Malinowski considered his theories of myth only to apply to "primitive" cultures, but that he latter extended the scope of his theories to encompass "modern" cultures, as well (Malinowski xviii). In the documentary, *The Hero's Journey*, Joseph Campbell also corroborates this attitude that myth is not only ancient, but modern, too. Campbell explicitly states that "myth has to deal with the cosmology of today... a mythological image that has to be explained to the brain is not working... then, you're out of sync" (Campbell 00:17:00). These perspectives argue that myths are still present in modern cultures, just that they may not necessarily take on the same structure as ancient or classical myths. However, it should be no far stretch to read the superhero narrative as a descendant of the heroic narratives of myth. Certainly, by interrogating the moral dilemma of security versus civil liberties in the superhero narrative, the values upheld in the story are strengthened and portrayed with greater value. The superhero genre flourishes off of its strong sense of right and wrong. Accordingly, readers of *Civil War* search for the moral values portrayed in such a dilemma. Furthermore, this binary system of right and wrong, good and evil imposes itself somewhat onto the debate between security and civil liberties, which leads the audience to see which one of the two bears more moral weight. Thus, if we look at the endeavours of superheroes as a type of heroic myth, then we see that Marvel Comics' *Civil War* reinforces both institutions and ethics, despite the surface ambiguity of the debate in question. The challenge to the traditional role of the superhero in *Civil War* does not alter the superhero's function; rather, it merely displaces some characters from being entirely deserving of the superhero designation. While Captain America and his anti-registration allies may have been breaking the law, it was an unjust law they broke and they defended their moral ideals. As such, it is easy to continue viewing these characters as heroic. On the other hand, Iron Man and his pro-registration allies have come close to being perceived as villainous as a result of their underhanded tactics. At the very least, they have lost much of their claim to being heroes. Although the Marvel superheroes are divided on the Superhuman Registration Act, there is still a dominant argument throughout the series. While the pro-

129

registration forces maintain the value of security and upholding the law, it seems that the dominant message is that of the anti-registration forces who defend the institutions of privacy and due process regardless of the law, because it is simply what is right. In light of this, the challenge to the traditional role of the superhero is rendered null and void. The role of the superhero remains the same – an upstanding beacon of moral justice – while those who can be justified in claiming the title of "superhero" has been altered through the events and actions of *Civil War*.

The debate between security and civil liberties is a complicated one. Although the victors of the tale are the pro-registration forces, the dominant argument in *Civil War* – the position preferred by the majority of readers – is the anti-registration position. In addition, the role of the superhero prevails as a moral beacon. Furthermore, the parallels between Marvel Comics' *Civil War* and the state of post-9/11 North America make it an interesting interrogation of the underlying concerns of our culture. Since this tale involves superheroes that function as moral role models, the debate between security and civil liberties becomes a caricatured battle of right and wrong. However, that does not diminish the poignancy of the arguments involved in the tale. Ultimately, Marvel Comics' *Civil War* crossover event appears to be a plea for people to re-evaluate the measures used in the War on Terror and suspicious legislation, such as the Patriot Act. In the sense implied by Malinowski and Campbell, *Civil War* and *Front Line* certainly function as modern myths that strive to regain a sense of morality in Zizek's era of paranoia.

CONCLUSION

The Superhero as Moral Guide

The Superhero as Moral Guide

In this interrogation of popular North American superheroes, I hope to have provided some insight into how the superhero acts as an influential mythical figure in contemporary culture. Throughout the previous chapters, this dissertation argues that popular superhero narratives must be regarded as modern mythology. Since ideals of justice are intrinsic to the structure of superhero narratives, it follows that people exposed to these narratives observe and learn these ideals as social norms. In investigating the superhero's role as a contemporary figure of myth, this project has been primarily concerned with three areas: an account of the history of the superhero from 1938 to present; an examination of the cultural functions of contemporary superhero narratives; and, an interrogation of vigilantism, responsibility, and justice in these narratives and how those concerns further relate to ideologies and practices in North American culture.

Superhero tales operate within culture as tools for moral education in the same manner as Plato and Bronislaw Malinowski understood myth. Modern superhero tales reinforce North American ideals just as the ancient tales of Heracles and Odysseus reinforced Greek institutions in the past. While the social mores reinforced by these tales differ depending on historical and social context, they nonetheless function to unconsciously support the institutions of a culture. Plato and Malinowski would likely interpret these iconic superhero narratives in the same way they have regarded myth. That contemporary superhero narratives are modern myths in North American popular culture has been the core, fundamental premise of my research, and thus it has been present in each chapter of this dissertation. And, as a means of concluding this

132

multifaceted interrogation of the superhero, I would like to take this opportunity to review the significant findings of the previous chapters.

As such, the chapters of the Golden section provide a historical foundation for the analysis that follows in later chapters. "A Brief History of the Superhero" is an overview of the history of the superhero from 1938 to present. There, I argue that there are three distinct paradigms in the history of the superhero genre:

TIME PERIOD	SUPERHERO AGE	CATALYST
1938 – 61	Golden Age	*Action Comics* #1
1961 – 86	Silver Age	*Fantastic Four* #1; Spider-Man
1986 – Present	Bronze Age	*Watchmen*; *Dark Knight Returns*

Despite the close ties between the history of the superhero and the history of comic books, the two exhibit unique, defining characteristics that differentiate their histories. The Golden Age of Superheroes begins with their introduction into popular culture. This period helped solidify the typical tropes of the superhero genre such that superheroes were characterized as costumed crimefighters and do-gooder adventurers, they have secret identities, they use their alternate superhero personae to fight crime, and they likely have superpowers of some sort. The superhero paradigm shifts when Stan Lee's superheroes usher in the Silver Age of Superheroes. His superhero characters demonstrated human failings, beginning with *Fantastic Four* #1 and epitomized with Spider-Man, and their narratives were written as serials with continuity – a radical change for superhero tales at that time. The Bronze Age of Superheroes revolutionizes the superhero paradigm by reflecting upon what it means to be a superhero or vigilante. Frank Miller and Alan Moore deconstructed the established tropes of the superhero genre,

133

challenging readers to confront the ethical issues inherent to the genre. This more mature mode of storytelling has since permeated the superhero genre across various media, thus defining the Bronze Age of Superheroes. In analyzing the nature of the superhero narrative, it facilitates understanding by recognizing the evolution of the superhero as evident in these paradigm shifts and as distinct from the history of the comic book industry.

In "Superheroes and the World War II Propaganda Monologue," it is evident that the superhero's emergence into mainstream popular culture bears a tightly woven relationship to the Second World War. Contrary to Will Brooker's claims, both Superman and Batman held a significant role in the North American propaganda campaign during the Second World War. This had a profound effect on the content of Superman narratives at the time. Although Superman's earliest heroic exploits held Marxist undertones, his character was forced to comply with the ideals of the propaganda monologue as the United States entered the war effort. Since the earliest, popular superheroes adopted such undeniable consumerist values, their following mythoi have built steadily upon those values. By focusing in on this historical moment as the superhero enters North America's realm of influential myths, it is evident that the narratives were directly affected by the political and social climate of the time. Not only were they affected by the social context, but they were employed as a means to affect the culture as well, as a medium to spread war-time propaganda.

The Silver section follows, reflecting the growth in the superhero narrative by adding theories of cultural analysis to my research. In "The Graphic Language of Superhero Narratives," I develop a semiotic analysis of prominent superheroes based

134

upon the theories of Ferdinand de Saussure, Roland Barthes, Umberto Eco, Will Eisner, and Scott McCloud. There, I focus my analysis on reading comics, the primary source of superhero narratives. To some degree, I argue, it is almost as if the images provide the semantics of sequential art, while the panels provide the syntax. Images communicate meaning through representation and gesture. Panels and gutters provide a system of combining the images like words in a sentence. Furthermore, through the combination of words and images in sequential art, the narrative attains a higher degree of successfully communicating the intended message of the writers or artists. The image communicates an enormous amount of information through its likeness and gesture, while the text can focus on dialogue or the thoughts of characters. Since the image can communicate the description of the scene, the characters, the action, and the emotional sentiment, the dialogue can focus on communicating discourse, ideas, and reflection. With such communicative force found in imagery, I argue that the notion of language is misrepresented when only speech and text are considered. Gesture, image, and sequential art represent a truly significant portion of language. Contemporary philosophy of language provides ample opportunity for imagery to be accepted into the public notion of the scope of language. While Wittgenstein emphasizes ordinary language use with the language game (Wittgenstein S7, S47, S65) and dynamic rule-following (Wittgenstein S83), Barthes helps us to acknowledge that meaning is communicated by innumerable means (Barthes 110). Together, Wittgenstein and Barthes bring attention back to the socially communicative function of language, thus allowing gesture, image, and sequential art within the scope of language. Furthermore, by applying the philosophies of Wittgenstein and Barthes to the analyses of Eisner and McCloud, it is evident that

135

gesture, image, and sequential art function as language. This is a vital understanding when examining the superhero narrative, since it has always been a very visual genre across multiple mediums.

That imagery is a potent means for communication is implicit throughout the following chapter, "The Superhero Narrative's Influence on its Audience." There, I argue that comics not only communicate a message, but that the message further has the potential to influence its audience. Accordingly, any censorship of the comics medium is an attempt to restrict the expression of undesirable influences to the comic book demographic. Studying the crusade against comics and Fredric Wertham's *Seduction of the Innocent* offers a wealth of information concerning freedom of expression and censorship. Through an analysis of the crusade against comics, it is apparent that art is necessarily communicative and that censorship is an attempt to regulate the artistic message according to a moral set, however imperfect that set of morals may be. While mass media is not the only environmental influence on a person's character, it is nevertheless an influence to some degree. This is a serious means of affect about which we ought to be more considerate since commercial advertising and political propaganda are constantly bombarding us in our everyday lives. Furthermore, this chapter argues that not only are superhero narratives carriers of influential messages, but other forms of entertainment, advertising, and journalism bear influence as well.

Finally, the Bronze section of my dissertation reflects upon the complexities of the superhero narrative as it stands today. "Justice and the Exceptional Character of the Superhero" examines the personality and nature of the superhero, and why they might act so heroic. By reflecting upon how the modern corporation is the epitome of the perfectly

136

selfish character discussed by Socrates in Plato's *Republic*, it becomes apparent how the superhero character is developed in opposition or defiance of such villainous characteristics. Neither Iron Man nor Batman have a legally binding contract to serve the public good, nor do either character owe any particularly large debt to society, and yet they both serve their communities, trying to uphold justice at great personal risk. They both attained the power to fight injustice from an abundance of wealth, intellect, and technology, which they gained from their close ties to their families' corporations. While both of these characters are exaggerated, they reflect real possibilities. Tony Stark and Bruce Wayne both experienced epiphanies, leading to the recognition of their duty to serve the public good. The superhero narrative can be read as an exaggerated narrative reflecting the choices we must make in our own lives. Such superhero narratives provide us with a noble example, however, exaggerated it may be, of what it might be like to live life justly.

In "Defending the Imperfect Utopia," I examine the various versions of utopia idealized by three of the primary characters of Alan Moore's *Watchmen*. This analysis of utopia in *Watchmen* identifies three forms of utopia – the unified utopia, the isolated utopia, and the status quo as utopia. Every utopia must be derived from a particular ideology; in a sense, utopia cannot escape moral relativism. Therefore, the capitalist utopia is just as valid a form of utopia as the socialist utopia, the free love hippy utopia, the Christian monastic utopia, or any other idealistic utopian construct. One of the most interesting notions of utopia present in *Watchmen* is Rorschach's vision of utopia. Rorschach resists the calculated slaughter Ozymandias employed to achieve utopia because Ozymandias' actions are incommensurable with Rorschach's unwavering

137

principles of right and justice. The utopian impulse which Rorschach seeks to defend is for a just utopia, not necessarily a capitalist utopia, although the two here coincide as the status quo utopia. Through Rorschach's attempt to defend his idea of utopia, we find an entry point into the American monomyth, as it is proposed by John Shelton Lawrence and Robert Jewett, and its correlative linking of national identity and utopian thought. This chapter further makes the case that the realm of utopian scholarship must be expanded to encompass a study of romanticizing the current cultural condition.

The final chapter, "Post 9/11 Discourse in *Civil War*," interrogates how cultural concerns regarding security and privacy can be reconciled with the traditional tropes of the superhero as a masked vigilante. Numerous events in Mark Millar's *Civil War* reflect events that have transpired in the real world since the attacks on September 11th, 2001, and the war on terror which followed. As people read *Civil War*, the usual search for the moral values, the binary system of right and wrong, and the battle of good versus evil imposes itself somewhat onto the ethically complex debate between security and civil liberties, which leads the audience to evaluate the moral arguments presented by each position. While the pro-registration forces maintain the value of security and upholding the law, it seems that the dominant message is that of the anti-registration forces who defend the institutions of privacy and due process regardless of the law, because it is simply what is right. The debate between security and civil liberties is a complicated one. Although the victors of the tale are the pro-registration forces, the dominant argument in *Civil War* – the position preferred by the majority of readers – is the anti-registration position.

With the three sections of my dissertation taken together, it is apparent that the superhero operates as a moral guide in North American culture. By extrapolation, the influence of the superhero tale in North American culture can be taken as a case study of media's persuasive influence within a culture on a larger scale to include other forms of entertainment, advertising, propaganda, and journalism. Accordingly, the arguments presented in this dissertation urge that academia bring the cultural influence of other popular narratives under a microscope and subject it to further critical reflection. Even amongst the superhero genre I would like to research further the issues of rhetoric in superhero narratives and the ideologies communicated through such narratives. Using my previous research as a foundation, I intend to further investigate the prevalent rhetoric in contemporary media, interrogate how rhetoric is used in superhero narratives, and reflect on how anti-hero protagonists affect the rhetoric employed. Everybody loves a hero, and I am fascinated by how the superhero narrative explores our cultural perspectives on heroism.

WORKS CITED

Achbar, Mark et al. The Corporation. Big Picture media Corporation. 2003.

Aristotle. On Interpretation. Trans. E. M. Edghill. The Internet Classics Archive. 21
March 2007. <http://classics.mit.edu/Aristotle/interpretation.1.1.html>

Baker, Nancy V. "National Security versus Civil Liberties." Presidential Studies
Quarterly 33, No. 3 (September). Center for the Study of Presidency. 2003. 547-
567.

Barthes, Roland. Mythologies. Trans. Annette Lavers. Hill and Wang: New York.
1972.

Beaty, Bart. Fredric Wertham and the Critique of Mass Culture. University Press of
Mississippi: Jackson, MS, 2005.

Brenzel, Jeff. "Why Are Superheroes Good?" Superheroes and Philosophy. Ed. Tom
Morris & Matt Morris. Open Court: Chicago. 2005. 147-160.

Brooker, Will. Batman Unmasked: Analysing a Cultural Icon. Continuum: New York.
2000.

-----. "The Best Batman Story: *The Dark Knight Returns*." Beautiful Things in
Popular Culture. Ed. Alan McKee. Blackwell Publishing: Malden, MA, 2007.

Campbell, Joseph. The Hero's Journey. Dirs. Janelle Balnicke & David Kennard.
William Free Productions. 1987.

Claeys, Gregory & Sargent, Lyman Tower, eds. The Utopia Reader. New York
University Press: New York. 1999.

DeTienne, Kristen Bell & Lewis, Lee W. "The Pragmatic and Ethical Barriers to
Corporate Social Responsibility Disclosure: The Nike Case." Journal of Business

Ethics Vol. 60. Springer Science & Media B.V. 2005. 359-376.

DiPaolo, Aeon J. "Wonder Woman as World War II Veteran, Camp Feminist Icon, and

    Male Sex Fantasy." The Amazing Transforming Superhero. MacFarland &

    Company, Inc.: Jefferson, NC. 2007.

Eco, Umberto. A Theory of Semiotics. Indiana University Press: Bloomington, IN,

    1979.

Eisner, Will. Comics and Sequential Art. Poorhouse Press: Paramus, NJ. 2006.

-----. Graphic Storytelling and Visual Narrative. Poorhouse Press: Paramus, NJ. 2006.

Evans, C. Stephen. "Why Should Superheroes Be Good?" Superheroes and Philosophy.

    Ed. Tom Morris & Matt Morris. Open Court: Chicago. 2005. 161-176.

Favreau, Jon. Iron Man. Marvel Studios. 2008.

Fingeroth, Danny. Superman on the Couch: What Superheroes Really Tell Us about

    Ourselves and Our Society. Continuum: New York. 2004.

-----. Disguised as Clark Kent: Jews, Comics, and the Creation of the Superhero.

    Continuum: New York. 2007.

Gordon, Ian. "Comic Books During World War II: Defending the American Way of

    Life." Comic Books. Ed. David M. Haugen. Greenhaven Press: Detroit. 2005.

Goulart, Ron. Comic Book Encyclopedia. HarperEntertainment: New York. 2004.

Greenberger, Robert, ed. Superman in the Forties. DC Comics: New York. 2005.

-----. Batman in the Forties. DC Comics: New York. 2005.

Harris, Stephen L. & Platzner, Gloria. Classical Mythology: Images & Insights 4th Ed.

    McGraw-Hill: Toronto. 2004.

Hebdidge, Dick. Subculture, the Meaning of Style. Ed. Terrence Hawkes. Methuen &

Co. Ltd: New York. 1979.

Heidegger, Martin. "The Nature of Language." On the Way to Language. Trans. Peter

    D. Hertz. Harper & Row: New York. 1971. 57-105.

Hughes, Jamie A. "'Who Watches the Watchmen?': Ideology and 'Real World'

    Superheroes." The Journal of Popular Culture. Vol. 39, Is. 4, 2006. 546-557.

Jameson, Frederic. Archaeologies of the Future. Verso: New York. 2005.

Jenkins, Paul et al. Civil War: Front Line #1-11. Marvel Publishing: New York. August

    2006 – April 2007.

Kripke, Saul A. Naming and Necessity. Harvard University Press: Cambridge. 1980.

Lawrence, John Shelton & Jewett, Robert. The Myth of the American Superhero.

    William B. Eerdmans Publishing Company: Grand Rapids, MI. 2002.

Layman, C. Stephen. "Why be a Superhero? Why Be Moral?" Superheroes and

    Philosophy. Ed. Tom Morris & Matt Morris. Open Court: Chicago. 2005. 194-

    206.

Magnussen, Anne. "The Semiotics of C. S. Peirce as a Theoretical Framework for the

    Understanding of Comics." Comics and Culture: Analytical and Theoretical

    Approaches to Comics. Eds. Anne Magnussen & Hans-Christian Christiansen.

    Museum Tusculanum Press: Copenhagen, Denmark. 2000.

Malinowski, Bronislaw. "Myth in Primitive Psychology." Malinowski and the Work of

    Myth. Ed. Ivan Strenski. Princeton University Press: Princeton. 1992.

-----. "The Foundations of Faith and Morals." Malinowski and the Work of Myth. Ed.

    Ivan Strenski. Princeton University Press: Princeton. 1992.

McCloud, Scott. Understanding Comics. HarperPerennial: New York. 1994.

Millar, Mark et al. <u>Civil War</u> #1-7. Marvel Publishing: New York. July 2006 – January 2007.

Moore, Alan, et al. <u>Watchmen</u>. DC Comics: New York. 1986.

Nead, Lynda. "From *The Female Nude: Art, Obscenity and Sexuality*." <u>The Visual Culture Reader</u>. Ed. Nicholas Mirzoeff. Routledge: New York. 1998.

Nietzsche, Friedrich. "Myth is Higher than History." <u>Philosophies of History: From Enlightenment to Postmodernity</u>. Eds. Robert M. Burns & Hugh Rayment-Pickard. Blackwell Publishing: Oxford. 2004. 150.

-----. "On Truth." <u>Philosophies of History: From Enlightenment to Postmodernity</u>. Eds. Robert M. Burns & Hugh Rayment-Pickard. Blackwell Publishing: Oxford. 2004. 150-151.

Nolan, Christopher. <u>Batman Begins</u>. Warner Bros. Entertainment, Inc. 2005.

Nyberg, Amy Kiste. <u>Seal of Approval: the History of the Comics Code</u>. University Press of Mississippi: Jackson, MS. 1998.

Perkins, Mike, et al. <u>Captain America</u> 23. Marvel Publishing: New York. 2006.

-----. <u>Captain America</u> 24. Marvel Publishing: New York. 2007.

Plato. "Cratylus." Trans. Benjamin Jowett. <u>Plato: The Collected Dialogues</u>. Eds. Edith Hamilton & Huntington Cairns. Princeton University Press: Princeton. 2005. 421-474.

-----. "Letters: VII." Trans. L. A. Post. <u>Plato: The Collected Dialogues</u>. Eds. Edith Hamilton & Huntington Cairns. Princeton University Press: Princeton. 2005. 1574-1598.

-----. "Republic." Trans. Paul Shorey. <u>Plato: The Collected Dialogues</u>. Eds. Edith

Hamilton & Huntington Cairns. Princeton University Press: Princeton. 2005. 575-844.

Rayment-Pickard, Hugh. "Suprahistory." Philosophies of History: From Enlightenment to Postmodernity. Eds. Robert M. Burns & Hugh Rayment-Pickard. Blackwell Publishing: Oxford. 2004. 131-140.

Reynolds, Richard. Super Heroes: A Modern Mythology. B.T. Batsford Ltd.: London. 1992.

Rhoades, Shirrel. A Complete History of American Comic Books. Peter Lang Publishing, Inc.: New York. 2008.

Rosenberg, Alex. Philosophy of Science: A Contemporary Introduction. Routledge: New York. 2003.

Schiller, Friedrich. On the Aesthetic Education of Man. Trans. Reginald Snell. Dover Publications, Inc: Mineola, NY. 2004.

Skoble, Aeon J. "Superhero Revisionism in *Watchmen* and *The Dark Knight Returns*." Superheroes and Philosophy. Eds. Tom Morris & Matt Morris. Open Court: Chicago. 2005.

Smith, Guy. 9/11: The Conspiracy Files. BBC. 2007.

Smith, Janet E. "Plato's Use of Myth in the Education of Philosophic Man." Phoenix, Vol. 1, No. 1 Spring 1986. 20-34.

Spiegelman, Art. Maus. Random House: Toronto. 1991.

Straczynski, J. Michael et al. The Amazing Spider-Man #538. Marvel Publishing: New York. January 2007.

Strenski, Ivan. "Introduction." Malinowski and the Work of Myth. Ed. Ivan Strenski.

Princeton University Press: Princeton. 1992.

Thompson, Don. "OK, Axis, Here We Come!" All in Color for a Dime. Eds. Dick
       Lupoff & Don Thompson. Ace Books: New York. 1970. 121-122.

Trushell, John M. "American Dreams of Mutants: The X-Men – 'Pulp' Fiction, Science
       Fiction, and Superheroes." The Journal of Popular Culture, Vol. 38, No. 1. 2004.
       Blackwell Publishing: Oxford. 2004. 149-168.

Wertham, Fredric. Seduction of the Innocent. Rinehart: New York. 1954.

Wittgenstein, Ludwig. Philosophical Investigations. Trans. G. E. M. Anscombe.
       Blackwell Publishing: Oxford. 2005.

Wolf-Meyer, Matthew. "The World that Ozymandias Made: Utopias in the Superhero
       Comic, Subculture, and the Conservation of Difference." The Journal of Popular
       Culture, Vol. 36, Is. 3. 2003. 497-517.

Zakarian, Scott. "Creating Spider-Man." Stan Lee's Mutants, Monsters & Marvels.
       Creative Light Video, Inc. 2002.

-----. "Here Come the Heroes." Stan Lee's Mutants, Monsters & Marvels. Creative
       Light Video, Inc. 2002.

Zizek, Slavoj. Welcome to the Desert of the Real. Verso: New York. 2002.

Lightning Source UK Ltd.
Milton Keynes UK
UKHW02f1836060618
323847UK00033B/469/P